How to Stop Overthinking

Keep Worry, Overanalyzing, Rumination, Intrusive Thoughts From Controlling Your Life, and Find Inner Peace

By Dean Bishop

© Copyright 2023 – Dean Bishop – All rights reserved

The content within this book may not be reproduced, duplicated, or transmitted without direct written permission from the author or publisher.

Under no circumstances will any blame or legal responsibility be held against the publisher, or author, for any damages, reparation, or monetary loss due to the information contained within this book, either directly or indirectly.

Legal Notice

This book is copyright protected. It is for personal use only. You cannot amend, distribute, sell, use, quote, or paraphrase any part, or the content within this book, without the author's or publisher's consent.

Disclaimer Notice

Please note that the information contained within this document is for educational and entertainment purposes only. All effort has been executed to present accurate, up-to-date, and reliable, complete information. No warranties of any kind are declared or implied. Readers acknowledge that the author does not render legal, financial, medical, or professional advice.

Table of Contents

Introduction 4
Chapter 1: Going Down the Rabbit Hole 7
   What Is Overthinking? 7
   Overthinking Versus Deep Thinking 8
   Why Do We Overthink? 9
   Ways That We Overthink 14
   How Common Is Overthinking? 16
   The Consequences of Overthinking 16
   Do You Overthink? 22
Chapter 2: Goal-Setting to Anchor Wandering Thoughts 25
   How Goals Help With Overthinking 25
   Key Principles of Goal-Setting 32
   Goal-Setting Techniques 34
   Other Approaches to Goal-Setting 45
   Tips to Maximize Your Success 48
Chapter 3: Teaching Your Brain to Exhale 56
   Stress and Overthinking: A Chicken-and-Egg Situation 56
   What Is the Anxiety Cycle? 58
   Getting to Know Your Anxious State 60
   Breaking the Anxiety Cycle 65
   Know Your Anxious State - Know What to Do 66
   Bringing Relief to Your Mind 68
Chapter 4: Essential Relaxation Techniques - From A(nxious) to Z(en) 95
   The Power of Shared Experiences 110
Chapter 5: Analysis Paralysis: Evacuation Plan 112
   What Is Analysis Paralysis? 112
   What Kind of Decisions Most Often Lead to Analysis Paralysis? 113

What Does Analysis Paralysis Feel Like? 113

Traits Associated With Analysis Paralysis 114

How to Beat Analysis Paralysis 116

Chapter 6: What Is Your Decision-Making Style? 124

More Is Not Always Better 127

Which Is the Better Style? 128

Decision-Making 101 129

Chapter 7: Rethinking Your Thoughts 138

Ways to Overcome Self-Doubt 144

Limiting Beliefs: The Beliefs That Hold You Down 146

What Is a Limiting Belief? 147

Change Your Limiting Beliefs Into Empowering Ones 151

How to Manage Your Cognitive Distortions 153

Chapter 8: Developing a "Free Your Mind" Lifestyle 160

Develop an Empowering Morning Routine 160

Develop an Empowering Evening Routine 163

Learning to Let Go 164

The Journey Beyond the Last Page 168

Conclusion 170

About the Author 172

References 174

Introduction

"I know I am not alone and more importantly, to all those like me who overschedule, overthink, overwork, over-worry, and over-everything, please know you are not alone."
~ Ryan Reynolds, Actor

Do you have trouble sleeping because your mind will not shut down? Do you spend a lot of time analyzing the meaning behind what others say? Do you frequently replay conversations in your head that you had with others? Are you often unaware of what is happening around you because your focus is on your self-talk?

These are just a few of the signs that may indicate that you have a habit of overthinking. I once had this problem when I was younger. I spent much of my time living in my head. I was constantly worrying about what others may be thinking about me. I replayed conversations I had with others repeatedly in my head, often interjecting what I wished I had said at the time.

These are just a few examples of the overthinking that I frequently engaged in. Only now can I appreciate the pain that I had self-inflicted on myself. My overthinking reinforced my feelings of self-doubt and created a challenge for me to be able to connect with others. All of these things took a toll on my self-esteem.

Overthinking took its toll on me in other ways, and if you are also an overthinker you probably can relate to this:

- Overthinking caused me to feel uneasy about happiness. After all, if I allowed myself to become happy, I would be letting my guard down.
- The self-doubt created by my overthinking negatively affected my relationships.
- My overthinking affected my ability to sleep.
- Because I could not let go of things, I was unable to enjoy the present moment.

Today, I enjoy a life where I mostly experience mental calm. However, this did not happen just because I "outgrew" it. What created this change was the fact that I was sick and tired of how I felt about my life. My overthinking had robbed me of feeling joy in my life. Despite having worked in the mental health field for over 20 years, I had to concede to myself that I was a victim of my overthinking. It was this realization that caused me to create a change within myself so that I could enjoy greater happiness in my life. And that is the reason why I wrote this book.

We live in a time when overthinking seems to be on the rise. In my daily life, I see how people seem to be more impatient, have more difficulty being still, and seem less aware of their surroundings. I believe this is partially due to our high-tech age. As a society, we are increasingly going online, whether it be for job reasons, research, or because we want a distraction from our lives.

Because of the speed at which information is presented to us, we have developed a need for instant gratification and our attention span has become shorter. The reason our attention span is getting shorter is that we are overthinking. However, it does not have to be this way. When you first wake up, is your mind not calmer than it is later in the day? You did not have to do anything for this to happen, it just happens. In this book, you will learn ways where you can develop a calmer mind while at the same time being more aware of what is going on within you and around you.

Overthinking is not a disease and hence, there is no diagnosis. It is simply a pattern of thinking that we adopted at some point in our lives. Given this, you can also discard this pattern and adopt a healthier one; mental calmness. If you are ready to commit to change, this book will show you the way. In this book, you will learn simple strategies for calming your mind.

Chapter 1:
Going Down the Rabbit Hole

"The easiest way to complicate things is to overthink." ~ Sukant Ratnakar, Quantraz

When faced with an important decision, it is not unusual for us to spend a lot of time thinking about it. I remember the time when I had to decide as to whether I was going to make a career change. I spent much of my time thinking about all my options and the benefits and consequences associated with each.

Now imagine what if this amount of thinking was not reserved for decisions of major importance. What if it was your normal way of thinking, even when it involved minor things?

What Is Overthinking?

Overthinking is the rumination of thoughts; it is when we dwell on our thoughts regarding situations at the expense of taking action to improve things. Further, overthinking is not reserved for situations of major importance. Overthinking can involve minor or mundane situations as well. Stated another way, overthinking can be described as unproductive thinking. Besides being unproductive, overthinking can disrupt your life and compromise your sense of well-being.

As I write this book, I remember what it was like when I engaged in overthinking. I would think about what will happen if my plans do not work out. I would anticipate what people would say to me before

I even met up with them. When I did meet up with them, I would think about what they were thinking of me!

During those years that I engaged in overthinking, I did not live in the world and experience it. Rather, I lived in my head and experienced my fearful interpretation of my life. It is for this reason that overthinking can be emotionally and physically draining. When we overthink, it makes it difficult for us to make decisions. Because we have trouble making decisions, we hold back on taking action, which then leads to anxiety. In turn, our anxiety makes it difficult to get a good night's sleep. All of this makes it difficult for us to focus and concentrate. This, in turn, leads to more overthinking.

When we overthink, we spend all of our time in our heads, so we miss out on the present moment, including our being emotionally present when we are around others. Our focus is on ourselves, not on other people.

Overthinking can be useful at times such as when you have to deliver on an important project. In this case, overthinking can get you motivated and more aware of what you need to do. On the other hand, it becomes unhealthy when it keeps you from taking action, disrupts your daily life, or negatively impacts your sense of well-being.

Overthinking Versus Deep Thinking

There is a big difference between overthinking and deep thinking. I remember a time when I had to make an important decision that would affect the well-being of my family. There were no easy answers, and there were many factors that had to be considered. This decision monopolized my attention, and I gave it a tremendous amount of thought. Though I was preoccupied with this situation, I was becoming more and more clear as to what the right decision was. It resulted in me feeling good about the decision that I made.

On the flip side, I remember what it was like when I was younger. How I handled difficult situations was very different. I felt stressed about the situation, and I repeatedly questioned myself. I overthought the situation, which resulted in me taking minimal action toward a solution.

These examples from my life illustrate the difference between overthinking and deep thinking. When you are engaged in deep thinking, you feel like you are moving forward in your understanding of the situation. Also, your thoughts are solution oriented. You are not dwelling on what may go wrong or in self-doubt.

On the other hand, overthinking leaves you feeling stuck and you are unable to make progress. Instead of being solution-oriented, your thoughts are focused on past disappointments or doubts about the future. In other words, your attention is less solution-focused and more focused on all the things that could go wrong. Instead of feeling more encouraged, you experience more negative self-talk, which leads to feeling anxious and emotionally exhausted.

Why Do We Overthink?

There are several theories on why we overthink. Some experts believe that overthinking is a strategy that we use to feel more in control and confident about a situation (Witmer, 2023). In our attempts to reduce anxiety, our brains go through all the possible scenarios and predict their outcomes.

Though overthinking may reduce stress in the short term, it usually creates greater stress for us in the future. The reason for this is that when overthinking, we are less likely to take action to address our situation.

There is also the theory that overthinking may be caused by past experiences. Children with overcontrolling parents are more susceptible to developing passive personalities, leading to overthinking. Also, those who experienced traumatic or stressful events in the past are more likely to demonstrate overthinking (Eng, 2020).

Lastly, there is the theory that overthinking may be a response from the primitive part of the brain. Overthinking, along with anxiety and depression, may be associated with the primitive part of our brain where survival instincts originate.

We retain a part of the brain structure that was found in early man and animals. For them, survival was the main concern. When there is a threat from a predator, there is no time for rational or optimistic thinking. Rather, there is a need for hyper-vigilance to survive.

Though we have evolved from our primitive past, and though we do not have to worry about being preyed upon by predators, that primitive part of our brain remains. Instead of predators, this part of the brain reacts to the threats posed by modern society, such as being able to pay our bills or relationship problems. Those who overthink may be caught in the fight-or-flight mode that is a response from the primitive brain.

Regardless of the reason why we overthink, that is not nearly as important as why we maintain this habit. The following are reasons why we may continue to do so:

Illusions of Certainty and Control: Despite all the disadvantages that come with overthinking, it does provide a benefit, though it is illusionary in nature. It is human nature for us to not want to feel uncertain; we need to feel that we are in control. Most of us need to feel that we are in control even in situations where things are out of our control. Ruminating thoughts and worrying may make us feel like we have a level of certainty and control although it is just an illusion.

The way of getting out of this trap is to learn to accept that there are times when there is nothing that you can do about a situation and to come to terms with that reality. It is beneficial to learn to live with uncertainty.

Perfectionism: Perfectionism is a personality trait; it is not a personality disorder. Those with this type of personality are ruled by their feelings. Intellectually, they know that nothing can ever be perfect. However, on the feeling level, they have difficulty moving forward because they feel like more needs to be done on what they are working on.

Those who are perfectionists often overthink a problem. They do this because they have a low tolerance for leaving a task that they feel could be improved upon. Overthinking distracts them from feelings that they are not good enough. For such individuals, it is important to learn to tolerate feelings of inadequacy so one can move forward.

Secondary Gain: The only reason why we repeat a behavior is because we perceive that there is a benefit to doing it. That benefit is a change in how we feel. While thoughts are not behaviors, our behaviors are often born from our thoughts. As we saw with perfectionism, overthinking can distract from feelings of inadequacy.

In the same way, overthinking can lead to other feelings that we find rewarding, even though it can lead to many negative effects in the long term. However, feeling good in the short-term is more impactful to the mind than the future long-term consequences, which remain abstract to the mind. By focusing on the long-term consequences of overthinking, you can train your mind to realize that short-term gain is not worth it.

Overgeneralizing: As previously mentioned, there is a difference between overthinking and deep thinking. Without recognizing that there is a difference, we may think that overthinking is a good thing. It should be clear by now that overthinking leads to more negatives than benefits.

However, even deep thinking can have its faults if it is overgeneralized. Just because deep thinking is useful in some cases, it does not mean it is useful in all cases. It is completely appropriate to spend time deep thinking when you want to figure out how to improve your relationships. However, deep thinking about whether you should exercise today or not just provides an excuse for not doing it.

You can avoid this situation by making a list of areas in your life where the only thing that is needed is to decide if you are going to do it or not rather than spending your time thinking about it.

Conflict Avoidance: We tend to avoid conflict. Most of us become fearful or anxious when a conflict arises. As a result, most of us have not learned how to deal with conflict effectively. Instead, we may engage in overthinking. The problem is that conflict is part of life. As long as we avoid conflict, we will just create more of it.

For this reason, use conflict as a learning tool for how you can handle conflict more effectively. With practice, you will feel more confident dealing with conflict, and you will be less likely to engage in overthinking.

Mental Health Disorders: Overthinking is not a mental disorder. However, overthinking is associated with some mental disorders such as anxiety, depression, insomnia, PTSD, and eating disorders (Witmer, 2023).

Childhood Experiences: For those who have a major problem with overthinking, the cause is frequently linked to childhood experiences that created a sense of uncertainty. An example of this would be a child who grows up with an alcoholic parent. In such cases, the child may engage in overthinking as a defense mechanism. As the child is uncertain how an intoxicated parent may react to them, the child may think of all the different scenarios that may occur to feel safe.

Culture and Thought: Our relationship with thoughts can be affected by our culture. An example of this is the difference between Western culture and some Eastern ones. In many Western cultures, we deeply identify with our thoughts. In other words, we personalize our thoughts, believing that our thoughts define who we are. In some Eastern cultures, where meditation and mindfulness are commonly practiced, one learns to observe their thoughts without personalizing them.

Occupation: Some jobs encourage overthinking. In such occupations, it may require a person to engage in thinking through multiple potential outcomes before taking action. Such environments may cause one to develop a pattern of overthinking.

Personality Types: Some personality types seem to be more prone to overthinking. Those who are very intelligent can jump rapidly from one idea to another. Being a quick thinker can lead to high achievement in life, but it can also lead to overthinking becoming a habit.

Ways That We Overthink

Cognitive distortions, which is a fancy word for overthinking, are distorted ways of thinking and there are five different types:

All-Or-Nothing Thinking: This is black-and-white thinking where things are either one way or the other but there is no in-between. An example of this would be a person who believes that unless they get admitted to a prestigious school then they are a failure. They have a hard time believing that they can become successful by taking other life paths, such as starting their own business.

Catastrophizing: This is the kind of thinking where we focus on the worst-case scenarios. When I was young, I would spend much of my time thinking about how I would never achieve the life milestones that others enjoyed, such as getting married or having a successful career. Today, I enjoy both.

Overgeneralizing: In this kind of thinking, we make broad generalizations based on small sample size. For example, someone may believe that all women are a certain way based on a few women that they know.

Jumping to Conclusions: This kind of thinking is similar to overgeneralizing in that we make a pre-determination about something being a certain way and that it will always be that way. Again, this kind of thinking is based on small sample size.

An example of this would be from my own life. When I was younger, I did not date much, and the few relationships that I had were short-lived. I concluded that I would never find a lifetime partner. Not only am I married now, but my spouse and I have been together for 20 years.

Mind-Reading: In this kind of thinking, you believe that you know what someone else is thinking without any evidence. I used to honestly believe that one of my co-workers was being arrogant and did not want to get to know me. I later found out that they were very shy.

Other patterns of overthinking may include rumination, which is when we obsessively think about something. Ruminating thoughts may include:

- Repeatedly thinking about the same concerns or fears
- Repeatedly thinking negative thoughts about the past or the future
- Continuously thinking about a problem when a solution has been identified
- Being unable to address an important issue because you are unable to move on

How Common Is Overthinking?

A 2003 study revealed that overthinking is very common, but more common in younger people. For the age group between 25 and 35 years of age, 73% engaged in overthinking while 52% for the 45–55-year-old age group. Also, overthinking was reported in females more frequently than in males (Eng, 2020).

The Consequences of Overthinking

To better appreciate how overthinking can negatively affect us mentally and physically, it is first necessary to understand the physiology behind the fight-or-flight response. The fight-or-flight response refers to when your mind and body are in a state of high alert due to a perceived threat.

Let us say you are about to cross a street when suddenly a car races by you. Without even thinking, you step back to the curb. When you first perceived the threat (the racing car), your brain sent a signal to your body to prepare for danger. Upon receiving the signal, your adrenal glands release the stress hormone known as cortisol.

Cortisol, and other stress hormones, affect the body by putting it in a state of high alert so that it is ready to fight or flee. Here are just a few of the many things that cortisol does to accomplish this:

- It tenses up your muscles.
- It increases your breathing rate.
- It increases your heart rate and blood pressure.
- It increases your blood sugar.

- It diverts blood from organs that are nonessential during an emergency and directs it to ones that are.

All these changes are what make it possible for you to react in an instant with greater speed and increased awareness of what is going on. When you are safe on the curb, and you had a chance to calm down, the cortisol level in your body decreases, which results in your body returning to its normal state.

Early in this section, I used the words, "perceived threat." The reason for this is that our bodies kick into fight-or-flight mode when we interpret a situation to be threatening, not necessarily if it is a real threat.

Overthinking creates stress, which the brain makes out as being a threat. When we habitually overthink, our bodies are routinely in fight-or-flight mode. In other words, we are creating chronic stress. When we experience chronic stress, the fight-or-flight mode does not have a chance to turn off. The body is not given a chance to return to its normal state. The following are specific ways that you can be affected by this:

- **Mental Consequences**

Anxiety: Overthinking leads to excessive thinking about the past and future. Further, our thoughts determine what we feel. Thoughts about past negative situations can bring about emotions of sadness or anger while focusing on thoughts of the future may bring about feelings of anxiety.

Depression: Overthinking can lead to depression if we dwell on our past. Many people focus on past disappointments or failures. In doing so, they crucify themselves by blaming themselves or feeling that their future will be just a repeat of their past.

Self-Esteem: Those of us who overthink frequently think about our missteps from the past and our concerns for the future. We also spend a lot of time thinking about worst-case scenarios. If that was not enough, we also give a lot of attention to things that are beyond our control. All these ways of thinking may take a toll on our self-esteem.

Insomnia: It should be no surprise that overthinking can make it difficult to fall asleep, which can lead to developing insomnia.

It is difficult to get restful sleep when your thoughts are racing. We need sleep to function properly the next day. While sleeping, your bodily functions slow down, allowing your body to relax and revitalize. Without restful sleep, these things cannot take place.

Memory Issues: There are two forms of memory, working memory (also known as short-term memory) and long-term memory. Working memory holds information that is relevant to what is happening to us at the moment. At some point, working memory becomes incorporated into long-term memory, where the information is stored.

For example, let us say you are learning a new language. In the beginning, the new words that you learn are kept in your working memory. At this point, you are aware of the new words, but you will probably forget them if you do not practice them. However, with continued practice, these new words become part of your long-term memory. Once there, you do not need to practice them anymore.

When we overthink, we are blocking our working memory. New information cannot enter it. As a result, it never becomes part of our long-term memory.

Slower Brain Regeneration: Overthinking creates stress, and prolonged stress can have a negative influence on the body's functioning, including the brain. While short-term stress can benefit us to get motivated, long-term stress can negatively affect the regeneration of brain cells.

Social Incompetency: There is a tendency for those of us who overthink to believe that others are being judgmental or critical of us. Having this assumption can cause one to feel uncomfortable in social situations. In most cases, we eventually find out that our assumptions about what others think about us were incorrect.

Increased Risk for Mental Health Disorder: Overthinking often involves putting excessive attention on our past mistakes and our perceived flaws. Studies have shown that ruminating on such thoughts puts us at increased risk of developing a mental disorder such as post-traumatic stress disorder, anxiety, or borderline personality disorder (American Psychiatric Association, 2020).

- **Physical Consequences**

Increased Blood Pressure: Overthinking creates stress, and stress can increase your blood pressure. In turn, high blood pressure can lead to strokes or heart attacks. Additionally, stress may lead to some engaging in unhealthy habits to relieve their stress, such as consuming alcohol or smoking. These behaviors create additional complications for the body.

Skin Disorders: The stress created by overthinking can play havoc on your skin. Stress can further aggravate skin disorders such as seborrheic dermatitis, dermatitis, psoriasis, and other diseases.

Change in Eating Habits: Overthinking can disrupt your normal eating habits by preventing the body's signal from reaching your brain. The body's signal informs the brain as to whether you are hungry or full. As a result, overthinking can cause people to lose their appetite or overeat.

Impact on the Brain: Overthinking alters the brain's functioning, which can lead to stress, anxiety, and depression. Additionally, it drains you of energy so that your ability to focus and make decisions can be compromised.

Digestive Problems: Given that overthinking leads to stress, overthinking can also affect your ability to digest your food properly. Stress can result in gastrointestinal problems, including irritable bowel syndrome and inflammatory bowel disease. Also, stress decreases the amount of blood flow to the stomach. Because of this, your stomach receives less oxygen.

Compromised Immunity: Stress, which is a byproduct of overthinking, results in the body releasing cortisol, a hormone that puts the body on high alert. This response is what is commonly known as the fight-or-flight response. Normally, when the perceived threat is gone, the body returns to its normal state. When overthinking becomes habitual, the body continually releases cortisol. When this occurs, the immune system is weakened, making us more vulnerable to being inflicted with disease.

Disruption of the Body's Chemical Balance: As mentioned earlier, our brains respond to threats whether that threat is perceived, or real. In other words, your brain cannot tell the difference between you believing that you are being rejected by another person and you being rejected.

By overthinking what others think about you, you are causing your body's stress response system to be overworked. The continuous release of stress hormones disrupts the normal chemical balance of the body.

Shortened Life Span: Prolonged exposure to stress can shorten your life span. When overthinking involves dwelling on one's fears and anxieties, the stress that comes from it can shorten one's life.

- **Personality Consequences**

Indecisiveness: Indecisiveness is also known as "the paralysis of analysis." When overthinking becomes habitual, we create more options for ourselves than we can handle. Not only do we create too many options, but we also get caught thinking of all the potential negative consequences that come from those options. As a result, we become indecisive. When we become indecisive, we also often become reluctant to try new things.

Creativity Suffers: Creativity occurs when the mind experiences moments of quiet, and you are not thinking about how to solve a problem. This is why our most creative ideas come about when we take a break from the situation or after a good night's sleep. The flow of creative energy becomes blocked when we spend our time overthinking.

Feeling Low in Energy: Focusing on specific thoughts requires more energy than random thinking. When overthinking becomes habitual, the consumption of mental energy becomes even more so. For this reason, those who overthink often feel fatigued.

Being Prone to Irritability: Overthinking creates anxiety, and anxiety can make it difficult to get a good night's sleep. In turn, the lack of sleep affects your sense of well-being. The result is often irritability, which can lead to further anxiety. It becomes a vicious circle, and it all starts with thinking too much.

It Can Be a Turn-Off: When we are obsessive in our thinking, it shows in our conversations with others. It can cause us to continually bring up the area of our concern, which can turn others off. Or we may not bring up our concerns, but our focus will remain on our concerns rather than what others are saying. This can make us seem disengaged or distant.

Do You Overthink?

Take the following quiz to see if you have signs of overthinking. When taking the quiz, keep track of all your "yes" responses:

1. In your mind, do you repeatedly go over conservations that you had with others? Do you look for evidence that you were misunderstood or that you offended someone?

2. When getting prepared for the day, do you take longer than necessary due to your need to look perfectly dressed?

3. Do you have difficulty making important decisions out of the fear of it not working out?

4. Do you obsessively go over the things that people have said to determine what they meant?

5. When you leave your home, do you repeatedly wonder if you forgot something or if you left something on?

6. Before having an important discussion with someone, do you repeatedly rehearse what you are going to say so that you will not goof up when you say it to them?

7. Do you rehearse in your mind how you are going to respond to another person and then are surprised when they do not respond the way that you predicted?

8. Do you have difficulty sleeping because you keep on thinking about what happened today or what might happen tomorrow?

9. Do you become anxious when someone does not reply immediately to your text when they have done so before?

10. Are you always preparing for the worst-case scenario?

11. Do you get distracted from what you are doing because you find yourself thinking about an embarrassing moment that happened years ago?

12. When using social media, do you constantly delete tweets or statuses out of fear that someone will take it the wrong way?

If you answered "yes" more than "no," you may be engaging in overthinking.

In this chapter, you learned all about overthinking. In the following chapters, you will learn how to rein in your thinking and strengthen your focus. We will begin with the power of goal setting, which is the topic of the next chapter. In Chapter 2, you will learn the different ways of goal setting so that you can achieve your outcomes.

Chapter 2:
Goal-Setting to Anchor Wandering Thoughts

"It is surprising how much free time and productivity you gain when you lose the busyness in your mind." ~ Brittany Burgunder

Imagine that you get a jar and fill it up with water and add sand. You then shake the jar and shine a flashlight at it. The light beam becomes scattered by the sand grains suspended in the water. You then set the jar on a table and let it sit for a while. When the sand grains settle at the bottom of the jar, you shine the flashlight again at the jar. This time, the light beam passes through the jar undisrupted.

What just has been described is a metaphor for the mind. The jar with water is a metaphor for the mind, while the sand grains represent thoughts. As for the light beam, it symbolizes attention or focus. The jar with the suspended sand grains is the mind engaged in overthinking while the jar with the sand grains settled at the bottom is a mind with clarity. It is through clarity that goals help us with overthinking.

How Goals Help With Overthinking

Unless we learn to focus our attention, we will be distracted by our thoughts. What gives goal setting its power is that it causes us to focus our attention. With a compelling goal, the light of our attention can shine through undisrupted by the scattered thoughts in the mind's waters. One way that goals help with overthinking is that they provide focus.

Goals and Focus: A compelling goal is like a target. One cannot determine if they are improving their accuracy when shooting a weapon unless they have a target. A goal that is properly structured provides a focal point for attention.

Just like when learning to shoot, goals provide us with feedback as to whether we accurately direct our attention. If we are moving closer to our goal's fulfillment, then we are accurately directing our attention. If we are not moving closer to our goal's achievement, it means we are not focused on the right thing. A goal is an intention that our minds create as to what we need to focus on. Without a compelling goal, our attention is directed toward the racing thoughts in our minds.

Goals and Clarity: The power of goals is that they provide clarity about your future. Goals are like a map that shows you the direction for turning your ideas into reality. They serve as a target for your attention so that you can direct your time and energy. Without goals, our lives would remain stagnant. Our lives would not move forward. Power comes from having clarity as to what you want for your life and what you need to do to achieve it. Goals provide that clarity.

Goals and Procrastination: All human behavior is guided by a pain-pleasure dynamic. We engage in behaviors that we believe will maximize pleasure or minimize pain. The reason why we set goals is that we believe that we will gain pleasure from achieving our goals. The reason why we procrastinate is because we believe that doing something will be more painful than if we put it off.

I tend to put off doing yard work because I am so busy. When I do have time, I prefer engaging in more enjoyable activities. I once received a notice from my homeowner association (HOA). I learned that I would be fined if I did not get my yard up to my HOA's regulations. Suddenly, doing yard work seemed more pleasurable to me than receiving a fine. For this reason, I stopped procrastinating doing yard work.

It is important to note that my procrastinating on yard work had nothing to do with the yard work itself. Rather, it was how I perceived yard work that caused me to procrastinate. My personal account points to the importance of understanding procrastination. You have the power to overcome procrastination by changing your perceptions of the task that you are putting off.

Changing your perception is particularly important when you are pursuing your goals. Whenever you sense that you may be taking your foot off the pedal when pursuing your goals, remind yourself of all the benefits that you would gain if you achieved your goals and the consequences you will have to face if you do not achieve them.

Goals and Motivation: I once had my own business as a photographer; my income was enough to support my family. However, it was not enough to get us beyond a life of living from paycheck to paycheck. I tried increasing my income, but it never panned out.

One day, we were hit with additional expenses, which would last long-term. I realized that we were in a real predicament. My current income would not be sufficient. It was then that I realized that I had to push myself. I needed to achieve my goal of increasing my income, even though I was unsuccessful in the past. The difficult position that I found myself in was a hidden gift because it taught me a vital aspect of turning goals into reality. What I am speaking of is motivation.

Goals are important for focusing one's attention on a specific outcome. This focused attention is what helps alleviate ongoing thinking. However, there needs to be something that drives and maintains that attention. Unless there is a driving force to do so, one may lose one's earnestness to achieve their goal. The drive that is being referred to is motivation. Goals are the target that we are aiming for while motivation is the fuel that drives us to take action until we have achieved our desired outcome.

Far too many people give up on their goals because they become frustrated when challenges are encountered, or their enthusiasm wanes. When my financial burden became greater, it was not difficult to find my motivation. I knew that I had to find a way to increase my business success. Not succeeding in doing so would be far too painful for me, which brings me to my next point. Motivation is all about the pain and pleasure dynamic.

All living beings are hardwired to avoid pain and pursue pleasure. A plant will change its orientation while growing to gain greater exposure to light. A bird will migrate south to avoid the winter weather, and an employee will increase their effort at work if given notice that their job is in jeopardy. Before the change to our financial situation, I tried to increase my business income but eventually resigned to the belief that I had done everything that I could.

When we experienced an increase in our expenditures, beyond what we could afford, then my marginal amount of comfort suddenly disappeared. What I was faced with was pain; the pain of knowing that I may not be able to support my family. That pain gave me all the motivation that I needed to be successful in growing my business beyond what I ever thought was possible.

A powerful strategy for moving beyond overthinking is to create a compelling goal for yourself. Your goal becomes compelling when you feel driven to succeed, regardless of what challenges you may face along the way. To find your motivation, you want to dig deep into your goal and find the motivating factor. You can do that by finding the purpose or the "WHY" of your goal. In other words, ask yourself why you want to achieve your goal. What will you gain if you achieve your goal? What would it mean to you?

Just as important is to ask yourself what the cost to you or your loved ones will be if you fail in achieving your goal. If you do not feel driven when answering these questions, it may be that either you are not digging deep enough into your goal, or you have not chosen a goal that is compelling enough for you.

What has been described so far does not mean every goal that you set needs to be compelling. However, those of us who overthink need to begin with compelling goals as such goals are more likely to hold our attention. As you start succeeding in attaining your compelling goals, you will have likely developed a more focused attention that will allow you to focus on goals that may be less compelling.

Goals and Self-Improvement: The desire for self-improvement is a natural part of life. Growth and expansion are the basis for living beings. Without growth there is regression. Plants and animals grow and mature. They also learn to adapt to changes in their environment. If we are not growing and improving, then we are declining.

What we refer to as a desire to self-improve is an expression of that impulse; it is the need for growth. As humans, we are placed in an envious position as we can consciously decide to improve as opposed to most animals, whose growth and adaptation are largely unintentional.

Goals are a product of this intentionality for growth. When we become intentional, overthinking is subordinated and replaced with a drive to succeed. By becoming intentional in how you live your life, your overthinking will gradually be replaced with a determination to grow. Goals are the product of this intentionality.

True fulfillment in life comes when we live by the philosophy of continuous improvement. By continuously working to improve ourselves, emotionally, mentally, and physically, we are abiding by the laws of life.

Goals Track Progress: A well-defined goal offers more than just a focal point for your attention. It also allows you to track your progress. Rarely does the journey toward one's goal achievement follow a straight line. Rather, it is more like a winding path.

Having a clear goal for what you want provides you with a focal point. By having a focal point, you can determine whether your actions are bringing you closer to your goal's achievement. If your actions are bringing you closer to your desired outcome then you are making progress. If your actions are not getting you closer to your desired outcome, you can adjust and try a different approach. In this way, goals provide a feedback mechanism for your actions.

Goal-Setting and Decision-Making: The guardrails on the highway keep cars from going off the road. Similarly, goals are guardrails for our thought. Goals keep you on track regarding your focus, time, and energy. Because you become more focused, you will make better decisions when opportunities arise. When you make better decisions, your actions and goals will be in alignment.

Overthinking and Complex Goals: Another way goals help with overthinking has to do with a certain kind of goal; complex goals. Goals can be simple or complex. With a simple goal, you have a direct path to achieving your outcome. An example of a simple goal is losing weight.

If your goal is to lose weight, there are not many steps that you need to take to lose weight. You just need to watch what you eat and exercise more. But what if your goal is to start your own business? To achieve this goal, there are numerous steps you need to take to achieve your outcome.

The following are just a few of the steps you would need to take:

- Write a business plan.
- Obtain the proper licenses and permits.
- Market your business.
- Purchase equipment and supplies.

Starting a business is an example of a complex goal as there are several steps that you need to take before you can achieve your outcome. For complex goals, you need to break down your ultimate goal, which is to start a business, into smaller goals. Examples of this are:

- Create a business plan by next week.
- Apply for a business license within the next three days.
- Research marketing ideas by next month.
- Learn how to write a business plan within the next two weeks.
- Create a list of needed equipment and supplies by next month.

You will achieve your ultimate goal when you achieve these smaller or sub-goals. However, it is not enough to just break your complex goals into smaller goals. You also need to prioritize your smaller goals. Going back to the previous example, I would prioritize my sub-goals as follows:

1. Learn how to write a business plan within the next two weeks.
2. Create a business plan by next week.
3. Apply for a business license within the next three days.
4. Create a list of needed equipment and supplies by next month.
5. Research marketing ideas by next month.

Breaking down complex goals makes you set priorities, which leads to better decision-making. In turn, setting priorities and making better decisions can help reduce overthinking.

Key Principles of Goal-Setting

Many people feel that their life is going nowhere. For some, the reason for this is that they do not know what they want. For others, they know what they want but do not know how to get there.

The way to get out of this trap is goal-setting. When you set a goal, you are setting a target for your future. Creating success in life comes from not only having goals but also understanding goal-setting. The following are the principles for goal-setting:

Commitment: Goals provide a target for your attention. However, there needs to be a commitment to reach that target. The commitment to achieve the goal must be there as obstacles are bound to show up as you work toward achieving them. It takes commitment to continue to move forward, though adjustments to your strategy may be needed. Without commitment, it is too easy to give up when the going gets tough.

Clarity: To be effective, goals need to be specific. Vague goals will likely lead to ineffective results. It is for this reason that goals need to be clearly stated. Clear goals are implicit, and they can be measured. When written this way, you will have a clear understanding of what is required of you to complete the task. In turn, completing the task increases motivation, which increases the chances of success.

Challenge: To be effective, goals need to be challenging yet achievable. Goals that are challenging increase performance and result in a greater feeling of achievement, which is motivational. However, it is a delicate balance. If goals are too challenging, it can result in frustration and in giving up. Motivation comes when we believe that the goal is challenging yet achievable.

Complexity: Goals that are perceived to be too complex can be discouraging and reduce motivation. When it comes to complex goals, it is important to have a realistic timeline to achieve the goal. It is better to find ways to simplify the goal to avoid becoming discouraged. You can do that by breaking down complex goals into smaller ones. Achieving your smaller goals will lead you to achieve your ultimate goal.

Feedback: Goals are most effective when they are structured to provide immediate feedback. When you have immediate feedback, you can tell if you are taking the right action for the goal's achievement and how you are progressing toward it. When you do not receive immediate feedback, you are unable to determine if you are taking the right actions.

Goal-Setting Techniques

The goal-setting technique that you use can be a game-changer in achieving success. As everyone is different, it is important to find the technique that works best for you. The following are different goal-setting techniques.

1. The Goal Pyramid

As stated earlier, the power of goals is that they provide a focal point for our attention. In doing so, they take us to go from overthinking to focused attention. There are a variety of different models for goal-setting, and the more detailed they are, the easier it is to focus on what needs to get done. Such a model is the goal pyramid.

The Two Types of Goals

In the goal pyramid, there are two kinds of goals, long-term and short-term. Long-term goals are goals that can take a year or more to achieve. Long-term goals involve major life areas such as family, career changes, lifestyle changes, and other broad areas.

Short-term goals involve goals that you want to accomplish within a few months. Examples of this would be losing weight or saving money to go on a vacation.

Subdividing the Two Goal Types

Long-term goals and short-term goals can be further subdivided into two groups. For long-term goals, those groups are lifetime goals and capstone goals:

Lifetime goals are major goals that you want to achieve in your lifetime. They are the kind of goals that are the answer to the question, "What do you want your life to be like in the future?" Examples of this would be being independently wealthy or traveling the world.

Capstone goals can be thought of as intermediate goals. In other words, they tie into your long-term goals. You need to achieve your intermediate goals first before you can achieve your lifetime goals. If your lifetime goal is to travel the world, your capstone goal may be to save enough money to make that trip possible.

Short-term goals can be divided into provisional and foundational goals. Provisional goals are stepping stones to achieving larger goals. For example, if your larger goal is to advance your career, your provisional goal may be taking a business course.

 Foundational goals can be accomplished in a year or less. They may be connected to your capstone goal, or they may stand alone. If your capstone goal is to attend graduate school, your foundational goal may be to apply to graduate school. If it is a standalone goal, it may be taking a course in martial arts.

The Three Layers of the Pyramid

Now imagine a pyramid that has three layers to it. At the very top of the pyramid are your lifetime goals. The second layer has your capstone and provisional goals, and the third layer has your foundational goals.

Think of the top layer as your mission goals. These are goals that you want to shape your future. Think of the second layer as your intermediate goals. These are the goals that will get you to the top layer. Lastly, think of the bottom layer as the task layer. These are the tasks that you need to do to get everything going, or they may be an end to themselves.

How to Use the Goal Pyramid

1. Now that the goal pyramid has been explained, you can use it to get your goals organized and clarified. To begin the process, make a list of all your goals on a sheet of paper. Here is an example:

    - Make a career change to the technology sector.
    - Take a trip to South America.
    - Refurbish my kitchen.
    - Learn martial arts.
    - Relocate to my home state where I want to retire.
    - Create a trust for my children.

2. After you have completed your list, determine at which level of the pyramid each item would fit. Here is an example:

Goal: Make a Career Change to the Technology Sector

This goal would be a lifetime goal as I am trying to create a new direction for my life. So, I would place it on the top layer; the mission layer. In placing this goal in the mission layer, I realize that something is missing from my list of goals. How am I going to achieve this goal? I need to get training in the tech field. So, getting training is a new goal that I need to add to my list. I will place this goal in the second layer, the intermediate layer because this is the layer where capstone goals go.

Goal: Take a Trip to South America

This is another lifetime goal, which would go on the top layer. As with my career change goal, I have neglected to include on my goal list a goal for how I am going to make that happen. I need to save money to make this goal happen. So, I need to add a new goal; save money for my South America trip. I would also put this goal in the intermediate layer.

Goal: Refurbish My Kitchen

If I already have the money to cover the refurbing of my kitchen, this goal will go into the third layer, as it is a foundational goal. I would place it in the task layer. Even if I did not have the money at this moment, I would keep it at the task layer if I can save the money needed within a year.

Goal: Learn Martial Arts

This goal would also be on the bottom layer of the pyramid, the task layer. It is a foundational goal that I can accomplish within a year, and it is not connected to a higher-level goal.

Goal: Relocate to My Home State Where I Want to Retire

This would be another lifestyle goal, so it would go on top of the pyramid. Given moving to another state requires a lot of preliminary work, I would need to create new goals that would make this goal possible. Examples of these other goals would be:

- Checking out the housing market in my home state
- Lining up employment if I do not plan to retire immediately
- Visiting my home state to check out the different neighborhoods

Goals such as these can go in the bottom layer. They are provisional goals because they are leading to a larger goal.

Goal: Create a Trust for My Children

This goal would be another lifestyle goal, so it would be on the top layer. However, to achieve this goal, I would need at least two more goals:

- I need to save money and invest it in the trust.
- I need to open a trust.

Saving money for investment would be a second-layer goal; it would be a provisional goal.

Opening the trust would be a third-layer goal as it is a task that simply needs to be done.

3. After you have assigned your goals to the different levels, the next thing is to prioritize them. Here is an example:

    Under my mission goals, which is the top layer, I have the following goals:

    - Make a career change to the technology sector.
    - Take a trip to South America.
    - Relocate to my home state where I want to retire.
    - Create a trust for my children.

    My next step would be to prioritize these goals. The way that I would prioritize them is by their level of importance to me. Additionally, I would have considered if some of these goals must be achieved before others can be worked on.

    Here are some examples:

    In terms of level of importance, I would prioritize my goals in the following way:

    1. Create a Trust for My Children: I want to start contributing to my children's trust as early as possible, so that comes first.
    2. Make a Career Change to the Technology Sector: Making a career change will increase my income, which will help me achieve my first goal. For this reason, it is second on my list.

3. **Relocate to My Home State Where I Want to Retire:** Relocating to my home state is third on my list because I want it to be achieved before I spend money on my trip.

4. **Take a Trip to South America:** Taking my South America trip is fourth on my list. I will have taken care of all my higher-priority goals, so now I can enjoy my trip without any regrets.

You would repeat this process with each layer of the pyramid. When you have completed this, you will execute your goals by starting with the bottom layer of the pyramid. As you complete the goals at the bottom layer, you would move to the second layer and do the same. Eventually, you would reach the top of the pyramid.

2. SMART Goals

Sometimes we set goals that lack structure. An example of this is on New Year's Eve you declare to yourself that you are going to lose weight. SMART Goals provide a structure so that your goal will contain the key elements that make goals effective. Those key elements are:

Specific: The goal is specific in that it states:

- What are you trying to achieve?
- Why do you want to achieve it?
- How will you achieve it?

Measurable: The goal is stated measurably.

Attainable: The goal is challenging but achievable.

Relevant: The goal is worthwhile to you. It is worth your time and energy.

Timely: The goal has a timeline to it.

The following are ways to turn "I am going to lose weight" into a goal statement that includes all five of these elements.

Original Goal:

"I am going to lose weight."

Original Goal Written as a SMART Goal:

"I will lose 30 pounds in three months by running and eating right. I will lose the weight because it will make me feel better about myself."

Rewritten this way, this goal is specific as it contains:

What are you trying to achieve?

"I will lose 30 pounds..."

Why do you want to achieve it?

"... I will lose the weight because it will make me feel better about myself."

How will you achieve it?

"... by running and eating right ..."

Besides being specific, it is also:

Measurable: "I will lose 30 pounds ..."

Attainable: I believe that this goal is attainable. I believe that I can lose 30 pounds in three

months.

Relevant: This goal is relevant to me because it will make me feel better about myself.

Timely: This goal is timely as I have three months to achieve this goal.

3. HARD Goals

If you have had difficulty in achieving your goals in the past, the answer to your situation may be using the HARD goals. Hard goals are designed to get you motivated and to achieve those goals that are important to you.

HARD is an acronym for:

- Heartfelt
- Animated
- Required
- Difficult

Heartfelt: Think about what achieving the goal would mean to you.

Animated: Picture in your mind what it would be like if you have already achieved your goal. Visualize it as vividly as you can. Try to incorporate all your senses when visualizing the achievement of your goal:

- What would it look like?
- What would it sound like?
- What would it feel like?
- Would you be able to smell anything?
- Would you be able to taste anything?

Required: If possible, link your goal to something that is required of you.

Example: If your goal is to start your own business, volunteer at an organization where you can get exposure to all its business aspects.

Difficult: When setting goals, it is important that you make them challenging. At the same time, you should believe that your goals are achievable.

4. WOOP Goals

WOOP goals are structured to create excitement, motivation, and a plan to achieve your goals. WOOP goals differ from other goal-setting methods because it is more execution oriented.

WOOP is an acronym for:

- Wish
- Outcome
- Obstacle
- Plan

As a goal-setting method, WOOP is particularly useful for changing habits.

Wish: Choose a goal that excites you and that you believe would make a real difference in your life.

Outcome: Imagine what your life would be like if your goal was already achieved. In your mind, see your goal being your current reality. Get in touch with the feelings that you are experiencing as you imagine this.

Obstacle: Identify potential challenges that you may encounter when trying to achieve your outcome. If your goal is to lose 30 pounds, what challenges may you encounter that could throw you off while pursuing your goal? An example of a challenge would be a behavior pattern of eating fattening foods when you feel stressed.

Plan: Develop a plan for how you will address those challenges, should they appear. For example, find an activity that you can use when you feel stressed that supports you in achieving your goal. Instead of eating fattening food, you could take a walk.

5. PACT Method

The PACT Method is best used for long-term goals that entail continuous progress to be achieved. However, the PACT Method can also be used in conjunction with other goal-setting models.

PACT is an acronym for:

- Purposeful
- Actionable
- Continuous
- Trackable

Purposeful: Purposeful goals are value-based. In other words, they are goals that are driven by your values. When you have a goal, try to determine what value it is meeting. If your goal is to change careers, what is it about the career that you are interested in that appeals to you?

Actionable: With the PACT Method, it is important to take daily action that will bring you closer to the achievement of your goal. If your goal is to become a black belt in karate, then each day you need to practice the different moves until you master them. The key is to focus on the daily action items rather than overthinking your ultimate outcome; becoming a black belt.

Continuous: Besides taking daily action, it is also important to experiment with different approaches to achieving your goal. If you are trying to invent a new product for the market, the odds are that you will not get it right the first time. You will need to try different approaches until you find the right approach.

When doing this, it is important to not be afraid of making decisions that may not work out. Additionally, it is important to not overthink what you are doing.

Trackable: This component refers to keeping track of the actions that you are taking as you work toward achieving your goal. Tracking your actions also allows you to look back at the progress you have made. Tracking is not intended to show you how close you are to achieving your goal. Rather it is to see how far you have come.

Other Approaches to Goal-Setting

Ask Yourself the 6 Ws: The different models for goal-setting have at least one thing in common, specificity. The more specific your goals are, the greater your focus will be. Regardless of which goal-setting model you choose, you can enhance its effectiveness by asking yourself these six key questions:

Who: Who will be involved in your goals?

What: What are you attempting to accomplish?

When: When do you want to achieve your goal?

Where: Where will you work to accomplish the goal?

Why: Why do you want to achieve your goal? (What will you gain from it?)

Which: Which resources will be required to achieve your goal? Which requirements and restrictions will you have to deal with to achieve your goal?

By asking these questions, you may gain awareness of factors, which you may have otherwise not considered, that may be impactful in achieving your goal.

Values-Based Goals: We are more likely to achieve our goals if they are meaningful to us, which is why using your values to drive you to achieve your goals can be so powerful. It is on this premise that value-based goals can be a powerful way to keep your attention on achieving your ultimate outcome instead of getting caught up in overthinking.

In value-based goal-setting, the objective is to link your goals to your values. For example, let us say that you have the goal of becoming more effective at your job. If you have taken on this goal because you fear that your job is at risk, you will be motivated by fear.

Being motivated out of fear does not always result in the best outcome because your fear may hinder your performance in some cases. However, if one of your deeply held values is that of giving or contribution, linking your goal to this value will result in your efforts being driven by a greater meaning.

The Backward Approach: Pursuing your goals backward can be an effective approach if you tend to overthink. When we have a goal, we normally have an ultimate outcome in mind, and we work toward achieving it.

The challenge is that we do not always know what steps to take to reach our goals. This kind of situation is fertile ground for overthinking.

With the backward approach, you do not try to figure out the steps to move forward. Instead, you start with your ultimate outcome and work backward to determine what steps are needed.

For example, let us say that you want to be promoted in your company. You would first find out what responsibilities and qualifications are needed to be successful in the position that you are interested in.

Your next step is to find out how you can meet those requirements. If it is work experience that is needed, you will look for how you can get a job in that area. If it is an educational requirement, you would find out how you can get admitted to the needed educational program. Getting the work experience and educational background may come with their own prerequires that you may have to meet. By working backward, you are taking an ultimate goal and breaking it down into short-term goals, which will eventually get you where you want to be.

By working backward, you can take a large goal and make it more achievable. This method can also be helpful if you are not sure what your goals are; you may simply know what kind of future you want. Using this technique will allow you to translate your vision into measurable goals.

One-Word Goals: While goal-setting models tend to work by directing us to become more focused, some techniques stress simplicity. Trying to find a single word that describes the outcome that you are striving to achieve. For example, if you are in sales and want to increase your income, your word may be "sales" or "connect." Repeating your chosen word may motivate and get you to focus on what you need to be doing.

Tips to Maximize Your Success

Regardless of what goal-setting model you decide to use, there are tips that you can use to increase your chances of success in achieving your goals. They are the following:

Write Them Down: When it comes to goal-setting, there is a power that comes from writing down your goals. Your chances of reaching your goal increase just by writing out your goals as opposed to thinking about them. The reason for the effectiveness of writing out your goals is not fully understood, but it may be that writing them out provides greater clarity, and clarity is power.

State Them in the Positive: When writing out your goals, state them in the positive. To illustrate this, here is an example:

"I will stop staying up late so that I can get more sleep." The way this goal is written is in the negative. It is indicated as such by the words "I will stop …" To state this goal in the positive, it may be written as "I will go to bed earlier."

Here is another example:

Negatively Stated: "I will spend less time worrying."

Positively Stated: "I will learn to calm my mind."

Make Your Goals Visible: I remember one night when staying up late to write an article for a client. I was doing this after having worked a full day at my regular job. My enthusiasm for writing was missing. I then happened to glance at my dresser where I keep a photograph of my wife. It reminded me about how much I love her, and how important my writing income was to keep us afloat. My self-pity quickly turned to motivation. Make your goals visible by finding an object that will remind you of the importance of what you are trying to achieve.

Go for Goals That Motivate You: Setting goals that motivate you will increase your chances of accomplishing them. Accomplishing your goals requires commitment. You will more likely stick it through if your goals are meaningful to you. When you find a deep enough meaning for achieving your goals, you can make accomplishing your goals a "must" rather than a "should." Doing so will increase your chances of achieving your goals as you will be less likely to put things off.

You can help find a deeper meaning for your goals by asking yourself, "Why?" Ask yourself, "Why do I want to accomplish my goals?" When asking this question, follow it up by asking yourself, "What will achieving my goal give me?" Or "What will I gain from making my goals a reality?"

Choose Goals You Can Control: We have two spheres of influence in our lives. The first sphere consists of those things that we can control. We can control our thoughts, actions, and words. The second sphere consists of those things that we cannot control. Examples of this would include other people and the environment.

The more that we can control the factors that are needed to achieve our goals, the more likely we will succeed in accomplishing them. If your goal is to lose weight, you will be in control of most of the factors that are needed to lose weight. You can control what you eat and how much you eat. If your goal is to start a business, there are significant factors that you cannot control, such as customer demand for your business or the state of the economy.

One way to increase your chances of achieving your goals is to set performance goals rather than outcome goals. If you are trying to lose weight, a performance goal would be eating the right foods in the right amounts. An outcome goal would be losing 30 pounds. By focusing on performance goals, you remain in control. You have more control over losing 30 pounds.

If your goal is to start a business, your performance goals would include things like:

- Choosing the kind of business that you want to start
- Writing the business plan
- Managing inventory

Outcome goals would be things like:

- Becoming a multimillion-dollar business
- Being the leader in your industry
- Expanding your business

You will more likely achieve your outcome goals if you focus on your performance goals.

Prioritize Your Goals: Achieving your goals requires focus. The challenge is that many goals are complex, meaning that they consist of several smaller goals. Building a house may be your goal, but it involves completing a series of smaller goals, such as coming up with the financing, to achieve it. In turn, these smaller goals may involve completing numerous tasks as well.

Handling complex goals can be a challenge for those of us who overthink things. For this reason, try prioritizing your goals and then focus on one goal at a time.

If your goal is to cook a gourmet meal, that goal would consist of smaller goals such as:

1. Gathering the needed cooking materials, such as pans and measuring cups
2. Purchasing the ingredients
3. Finding the recipe
4. Cooking the meal

With such a goal, you would prioritize these smaller goals, as shown here:

1. Finding the recipe
2. Purchasing the ingredients
3. Gathering the needed cooking materials, such as pans and measuring cups
4. Cooking the meal

After prioritizing the goals, focus on one goal at a time. When you have achieved the first goal, move on to the next one.

Develop Mini Goals: There are certain situations where you have multiple objectives that you are trying to achieve. An example of this would be in business or making a lifestyle change. Meeting those objectives may seem overwhelming, and it can lead to overthinking. In these kinds of situations, it is helpful to break down those objectives into mini-goals. The development of mini-goals will provide a framework for the ultimate outcome that you are trying to achieve.

By developing mini goals, you will make achieving your ultimate outcome seem easier. Mini goals are easier to manage, and you will be able to see the results of your efforts sooner. If your goal is to create a lifestyle change, there are numerous objectives that you need to consider. Some of these include:

- Your relationships
- Your physical health
- Your emotional health
- Your career or professional life
- Your finances

Each of these life areas can contain smaller goals. For example, for physical health:

- Eat healthier.
- Exercise more.
- Get more sleep.

By meeting these smaller goals, you achieve the larger goal, physical health. By following this same process with the other life areas, you will achieve your ultimate goal, creating a lifestyle change.

Anticipate the Obstacles: Anytime that you pursue a worthwhile goal, you are bound to encounter obstacles. When this happens, we may get discouraged and may even give up pursuing our goals. Instead of getting caught off guard by obstacles, it is better to anticipate them in advance. Think of the potential obstacles that you may face while working toward your goal's achievement. For each potential obstacle, think of ways that you can overcome it.

See Your Future in Advance: As often as you are able, visualize your goal as being your current reality. Make your visualizations as detailed as you can. See yourself thinking and doing the things that you would be doing if you were experiencing your goal today.

Remember Your WHY: Knowing your "WHY" will provide your motivation. Continuously remind yourself of what achieving your goal would mean to you. How would your life be different if you achieved your goal?

Reward Yourself: All behavior is based on cost and benefits. If you engage in behavior that results in negative consequences, you are less likely to repeat that behavior. If the behavior results in a positive outcome, we will be more likely to repeat that behavior in the future. It is for this reason that it is important that you reward yourself anytime you take an action that brings you closer to achieving your goal.

Creating changes in behavior involves reinforcing that behavior at the time that it occurs. What this means is that you should reward yourself the moment that you catch yourself doing something right. If your goal is to lose weight, reinforce yourself the moment that you make a decision not to eat the foods that tempt you.

Reinforcement of behavior is less effective if you postpone rewarding yourself. Think of ways that you can instantly reward yourself. One way is to tell yourself, "Good job!" or something like that. Later, you can give yourself a larger reward, such as treating yourself to a nice dinner.

Hold Yourself Accountable: Holding yourself accountable is a proven way to increase goal achievement. Find someone who will be honest with you and hold you accountable and ask them if you can use them as an accountable partner. Let them know about the goal that you have set and check in with them regularly to let them know about the progress you are making toward achieving your goals.

Give Yourself a Deadline: An effectively stated goal includes a deadline. You need a target date for when you plan to achieve your goals. The following is a goal stated in two different ways, the first is without a timeline and the second is with one:

- I will lose 30 pounds
- I will lose 30 pounds in three months

By giving yourself a deadline, you create a sense of urgency within you and expectation for when you will need to achieve it. If things do not work out, and you do not meet your deadline, that is okay. Evaluate why the deadline was not reached and set a new deadline. Lastly, it is important that you give yourself a realistic timeline to achieve your goals. Not giving yourself enough time will only lead to you becoming frustrated.

Monitor Your Progress: I remember when I went hiking on a mountain trail, and I reached a point where I had doubts as to whether I could continue. I was tempted to give up and go back to the bottom of the mountain. I was turning around so that I could make my way back down when I saw how far I had come to be where I was standing. Seeing what I had accomplished already gave me a whole new perspective on things, and I was able to complete my hike to the top.

Just as in hiking, it is important to take a moment to review what you have accomplished already. When we are so fixed on achieving our outcome, we often lose sight of how far we have come. Naturally, it also occurs the other way. You may look back at what you accomplished and realize that you have made little headway. If this occurs, you have a chance to evaluate what you can improve or change your approach entirely.

Take the time to learn from your successes and failures in achieving your goals. By doing so, you may find patterns in your thinking that make a difference in future goal-setting endeavors.

Reach Out to Others: We all need help now and then. When you are unsure as to what to do, or you are feeling stuck, talk to someone who may be able to give you advice. Getting encouragement or a different perspective on how to approach your situation can make a difference as to whether you achieve your goals.

In this chapter, we explored how we can better focus on our goals. In the next chapter, you will learn how to control your focus to calm your mind.

Chapter 3:
Teaching Your Brain to Exhale

"Rule number one is, do not sweat the small stuff. Rule number two is, it is all small stuff."
~ Robert Eliot

In Chapter 2, the metaphor of the jar filled with water and sand was given. When shaken, the sand clouds the water. When the jar is allowed to sit, the sand settles and the water becomes clear. This chapter is about learning how to clear the waters of our minds. But before discussing how to clear your mind, it is important to first understand the effects of stress and anxiety on overthinking.

Stress and Overthinking: A Chicken-and-Egg Situation

Most of us are familiar with the expression, "The chicken or the egg?" The phrase refers to the question of which came first. Stress and overthinking fit the "chicken or the egg?" category. Which came first, stress or overthinking? The answer to that question is that they are the product of each other. It is for this reason that many of us have difficulty stopping our endless thinking. We are either focusing on the stress or the overthinking when both need to be addressed.

To understand the dynamics of stress and overthinking, it is helpful to first understand the nature of our minds and bodies. As with animals, our bodies have a stress response system, commonly known as the "fight-or-flight response." The stress response system refers to how the mind and body interact at times when there is a perceived threat.

Early on in the history of our species, we faced the threat of being attacked by hungry predators or warring tribes. When faced with such a threat, our brains send a message to the body for it to release stress hormones, such as cortisol. These hormones target specific organs that are needed when faced with imminent danger. The heart beats faster, blood pressure rises, muscles tense, and we become more alert.

These changes are what we experience as stress, and they put the mind and body on high alert so that we can deal with the threat. When the threat is over, the body's chemistry returns to normal functioning.

In our modern times, the risk of being attacked by a hungry predator or a warring tribe is no longer a concern. However, our stress response is doing overtime. How can that be? The reason for it is that the stress response system does not just respond to actual threats. It also responds to perceived threats. Anytime we interpret a situation to be threatening, the stress response system is activated.

Hungry predators and warring tribes have been replaced by running late for appointments, getting caught in a traffic jam, or going on a first date. Anything that you experience as being emotionally or physically threatening will activate your stress response system.

Now that we understand the stress response system, it is time to see how stress and overthinking are interrelated to each other. Let us say that you have a troubling thought about something. You wonder if you turned off the stove when you left your home. That thought is a perceived threat.

The brain detects that threat and triggers the body to release stress hormones. Your body chemistry changes, resulting in you feeling stressed. Your body feels stressed, and your mind responds by overthinking. You are thinking about all things that are going wrong or could go wrong. This in turn keeps your stress response system operating. Because it continues to operate, you continue to overthink. All of this leads to feelings of anxiousness, which has its own cycle.

What Is the Anxiety Cycle?

I remember as a child my science teacher did a demonstration for our class. He placed a magnet on a piece of paper and then placed iron filings around the magnet. I watched as the magnet attracted the iron filings to it. In a way, our thoughts are like this as well. When you place your attention on a thought, it will attract other thoughts of like kind.

If your attention is placed on a worrisome thought, that thought will attract other worrisome thoughts. These worrisome thoughts will build on your original thought.

For example, you may think to yourself, "I sure hope my job interview goes well; I really need this job!" This thought may attract other thoughts, such as, "What if I say the wrong thing during the interview?" In turn, these thoughts may attract other thoughts, such as, "What if do not get the job? How will I pay my bills?"

Each negative thought attracts other thoughts that are of the same nature. The reason for this is we experience what we focus on. If you focus on fear-based thoughts, you will attract other similar thoughts. When this occurs, we may find ourselves in an anxiety cycle.

The anxiety cycle refers to the phases we go through when we avoid dealing with our anxious feelings. There are four stages to the anxiety cycle:

Stage 1. The Desire to Stop Feeling Anxious: Step 1 of the anxiety cycle is the same thing as the fight-or-flight response. You are in a situation that you find intimidating, and you are trying to find a response to relieve yourself of your anxious feelings.

Example of Stage 1: Your supervisor asks you to give a presentation to your team. The idea of speaking before your coworkers makes you feel anxious.

Stage 2. Trying to Avoid the Situation That Is Causing You to Feel Anxious: This is the stage where the symptoms of anxiety appear, and you try to avoid experiencing them. These symptoms include things like anxious thoughts, anxious feelings, tenseness, and high blood pressure. We commonly make the mistake of trying to avoid the situation that we believe is causing us to become anxious when we are trying to avoid experiencing the symptoms of anxiety.

We have attributed our anxious feelings to the situation. In truth, our anxiousness comes from how we think about the situation. Many people have a fear of snakes and become anxious just by thinking about them. Yet, some people are fascinated by snakes and enjoy keeping them.

Snakes do not cause anxiety, rather anxiety is caused by the perception that we have of snakes. We may think that we are avoiding snakes when in fact we are trying to avoid the anxious feelings that we experience when we think about snakes.

Example of Stage 2: To avoid your anxious feelings, you start thinking of ways that you can avoid giving the presentation, such as calling in sick.

Stage 3. Experiencing Temporary Relief: This is the stage where you are trying to think of ways to avoid experiencing feelings of anxiety.

Example of Stage 3: You decide to go with your plan of calling in sick, which gives you a sense of relief.

Stage 4. Returning to an Anxious State: Because we often avoid situations that caused us to feel anxious, we neglected to learn how to manage our reactions to the situation. For this reason, we continue to feel anxious. We have not learned how to manage our anxiety. Our anxiety continues to take a toll on us, leaving us feeling mentally, emotionally, and physically fatigued.

Example of Stage 4: When you return to work, you find out that you have been assigned to give the presentation on another date. Hearing this causes you to return to an anxious state.

Getting to Know Your Anxious State

Before we can learn to manage our anxiety, we first need to know how we experience anxiousness. Now that you have learned about the different stages of the anxiety cycle, the next step is to understand your anxiety response. To do this, do the following steps:

Step 1. Checking Your Response

The first step to getting to know your anxious state is to understand how you react when feeling anxious. You can do this by asking yourself the following questions:

- What did you experience that led you to feel anxious? Was it a specific event, a thought, an image, a memory, or a feeling?
- How did you experience your feelings of anxiousness? Was it a thought, a sensation, or something else?
- How did you respond when you experienced signs of anxiousness? What did you do?

Step 2. Reflect on Your Thinking

After having identified how you react to anxiousness, the next step is to reflect on your thinking. Do this by asking yourself the following questions:

Were you engaged in negative thinking when you felt anxious? Negative thinking can include any of the following:

- Overthinking
- Being obsessed with negative thoughts
- Thoughts of self-doubt
- Catastrophizing, which is when focus on the worst-case scenario

The problem is not that we experience negative thoughts; the problem is that they become the object of our attention. We experience what we focus on. If you experience a negative thought, acknowledge it and then shift your focus to what you want to happen. You can do this by asking yourself empowering questions.

Let us say you are preparing for a job interview, and a thought appears, "What if I do not come across as being confident?" Instead of getting caught up in this thought, as yourself questions like the following:

"What can I do to feel more confident?"

"What can I focus on that will make me feel more relaxed?"

"What can I tell the interviewer to demonstrate the value that I can bring to the position?"

When you focus your attention on these kinds of questions, you will attract other similar thoughts. The only difference is that they will empower you rather than disempower you. The key to breaking out the anxiety cycle is to take charge of your focus.

Step 3. Perform a Body Scan

After checking in with your thoughts, the next step is to check in with your body. You can do that by doing a body scan. Place your attention on your experience of the body. Notice what you are experiencing in your body. Look for things like:

- Bodily sensations such as tension or numbness
- Stomach discomfort
- Increased heart rate
- Increased blood pressure
- Sweating

Step 4. Identify Your Coping Strategy

Anxiety is created when the focus of our attention is on negative thoughts. In turn, these negative thoughts attract other similar thoughts. Unfortunately, we often try to deal with our anxious feelings in a manner that only perpetuates our anxiety. The following are ways that we commonly use to deal with our anxiety that only make it worse:

Avoidance: Instead of dealing with the cause of our anxiety, we may avoid it. The problem is that avoiding the cause of our anxiety does not do anything to improve the situation. It may make things even worse. The reason for this anxiety is energy.

Just because we avoid the anxiety-causing situation does not mean that this energy disappears. Instead, it remains dormant within us. In doing so, it may appear in other ways. For example, I may avoid engaging in social situations with other people because that creates anxiety in me. Even though I may avoid other people, my anxiety remains with me. Because of this, I may have trouble sleeping at night, or I may experience racing thoughts.

Safety Behaviors: There are times when we are unable to avoid anxious-causing situations. When faced with such situations, we may turn to safety behaviors. Safety behaviors are behaviors that we engage in to lower our anxiety. The problem is that safety behaviors only work in the short term. In the long term, they will make our anxiousness even worse.

Let us say that I become anxious in large social gatherings. One day, I must attend a large wedding. Because it is the wedding of a family member, I am unable to avoid it. When I attend the wedding, I resort to using my safety behaviors. Let us say my safety behavior is to remain in the proximity of one of my siblings. For the entire event, I never leave my sibling's side. If I stay by my sibling's side, my anxiety remains at a manageable level.

The problem with my safety behavior is that it creates in me the illusion that the only reason why I did not feel anxious during the wedding is because I stayed with my sibling. By sticking with my safety behavior, I never provide myself the opportunity to challenge my anxiety on my own terms. Because of this, I will continue to depend on my sibling in the future when I need to attend a social setting. I miss out on proving to myself that I can do it on my own. For this reason, my anxiety will continue. Safety behaviors can also work against you in another way as they can become a self-fulfilling prophecy. If I resort to using my safety behavior every time I attend a large social gathering, I am anticipating that I will become anxious. Because I am anticipating I will be anxious, I become anxious.

The following are other examples of safety behaviors:

- Remaining silent when others are engaging in conversation
- Not making eye contact
- Not leaving the side of someone whom you know
- The use of alcohol or drugs

To break your dependency on safety techniques, it is important to push yourself and allow yourself to experience your anxiety for a short while, without the use of your safety techniques. By letting yourself experience anxiety, without making any judgments about the situation, you will come to realize that anxiety is a feeling that we sometimes experience.

As with other feelings, anxiety cannot harm you. It has no inherent power of its own. It is our fear of becoming anxious that causes us to become anxious. As you learn to accept your feeling of anxiety, your physical symptoms will begin to lessen.

Breaking the Anxiety Cycle

In the last four steps, you got to know how you experience and react to anxiousness. In doing so, you got to know your anxiety cycle. It is now time to break that cycle so that you respond to anxious feelings in a way that empowers you rather than recycling your old fears. The following is a range of techniques for breaking your anxiety cycle:

Reversing the Anxiety Cycle

One way of reversing the anxiety cycle is to reverse the steps of the anxiety cycle. As a reminder, the steps to the anxiety cycle are:

Stage 1. The desire to stop feeling anxious

Stage 2. Trying to avoid the situation that is causing you to feel anxious

Stage 3. Experiencing temporary relief

Stage 4. Returning to an anxious state

The revised steps for the anxiety cycle are as follows:

Step 1. Confront Your Fears: Confront your fears without using your safety behaviors or any other disempowering coping strategies.

Step 2. Embrace the Feeling: Embrace your feelings of anxiousness; do not try to resist them. Allow yourself to feel them. If your anxiety levels increase slightly, that is okay. You only have to do this step for a few minutes. The main thing is that you want to be able to experience your anxious feelings and realize that these feelings cannot harm you. As you stay with the anxious feelings, they should decrease in intensity.

Step 3. Learn Healthy Coping Skills: Coping skills differ from safety techniques in that they allow us to manage our anxiety while we face our challenges. Referring to the previous example, staying in the proximity of my sibling is a safety technique. It does not do anything to help me overcome my anxiety as it prevents me from facing it.

What if I tried to manage my anxiety as I exposed myself to a large social setting? What if I used deep breathing exercises to manage anxiety while I was in that kind of environment? If did things like that, I would be utilizing healthy coping skills. I am not trying to avoid the source of my anxiety. Rather, I am regulating my anxiety level so that I can learn to overcome my fears.

Step 4. Take Control: Remember, you are in control of your reactions and responses. The reason why you became anxious over the situation is because of what you were telling yourself. It is how you saw the situation rather than the situation itself. By remembering that you can create empowering meanings for any situation, you can reduce your anxiety levels. Besides breaking the anxiety cycle, you can also bring relief to your mind by challenging your concerns, which are discussed in the next section.

Know Your Anxious State - Know What to Do

The term "fight-or-flight response" is often used to describe a situation when an animal is facing a threat. The animal will either defend itself by fighting, or it will flee to safety. The fight-or-flight response is the mechanism that the mind and body use for the survival of the organism. This same mechanism is found in humans. Instead of being triggered by the sight of a predator, our fight-or-flight response can be triggered by an argument or work stress.

When the fight-or-flight response is activated, changes in our physiology occur so that our minds and bodies are put in a state of high alert. Some of these changes include increased muscle tension, blood pressure, and heart rate.

While everyone experiences the same physiological changes, how we respond to stress outwardly can differ from person to person. There are three ways that we outwardly respond to stress. By identifying how you respond, you can more effectively reduce your stress.

Becoming Over-Excited: With this response, you become angry, overly emotional, or agitated. If this is your response style, engage in activities that you find calming.

Becoming Under-Excited: In this response, you become withdrawn or depressed. You may also feel like your spaced out due to the stress. If this describes you, engage in activities that are energizing and stimulating.

Becoming Immobilized: With this response, you feel frozen in that you are unable to take action to deal with the situation. This kind of response is frequently associated with those who have a history of trauma. If this describes you, you need to engage in physical movement that involves your arms and legs. Do things like swimming, walking, running, or dancing. By focusing on your bodily sensations, you will remove your focus from your thoughts.

Bringing Relief to Your Mind

So far in this chapter, a general overview has been provided as to how stress, overthinking, and anxiety can create distress in our minds. In Chapter 4, you will learn how practicing mindfulness and meditation can help you calm your mind.

Both mindfulness and meditation help depersonalize our thoughts. In other words, we often personalize our thoughts, meaning that we take our thoughts personally. We may tend to accept them without questioning their validity.

Fortunately, you do not have to wait till Chapter 4 to challenge your thoughts as you can start doing it now. The following is a list of techniques that you can use to bring relief to your mind:

Challenge Your Thinking: A common challenge that comes with overthinking is that we may not take the time to question the validity of our thinking. Instead, we may assume that our thoughts are based on reality. It is important to question the validity of your thoughts as it can liberate you from the false notions that you may have about yourself and your world.

Question Your Concerns: When you start to overthink and find yourself getting caught up in worrisome thoughts, challenge their validity by responding to the following questions in your journal:

For all of my past worries, how many came to be true?

We can worry about so many things. We use up so much energy worrying, not to mention the suffering that we cause ourselves. However, our worries frequently do not come to fruition.

If the situation that I am worried about did come to be, what would be the worst-case scenario? What would be the best-case scenario? What is most likely to happen?

When it comes to our worries, we often overthink. We think of all the different ways that things could go wrong. Instead of letting your imagination go wild, you take a more balanced view of your concerns.

Is that which I am worried about within my control? If so, what can I do to improve the situation? If it is not within my control, what can I do to feel better about the situation?

Often, the things that we worry about are not within our control. If this is the case, what good will worrying do? Worrying about something that is out of your control is like putting yourself in double jeopardy. Not only are dealing with your concerns for the future, but all your worrying will take a toll on you.

If that which you are worrying about is in your control, then act so that you can deal with the situation. If that which you are worrying about is not in your control, then find ways to deal with your fear. In either case, worrying is a waste of energy.

If I journaled today about this thing that I am worried about, how do I think I would feel when I read about it tomorrow?

When you write down what you are feeling, you will often find that you feel a sense of release. The reason for this is you are purging yourself of the thoughts and feelings that you are holding regarding the issue that you are facing. When you combine this with time, the impact of our concerns may further lighten.

When you have responded to these questions in your journal, I recommend that you reread what you wrote the following day. Doing so will likely provide you with a new perspective on the situation. If you feel it is needed, continue to journal about it.

Asking Empowering Questions: Let us say you are preparing for a job interview, and a thought appears, "What if I do not come across as being confident?" Instead of getting caught up in this thought, ask yourself questions like the following:

- "What can I do to feel more confident?"
- "What can I focus on that will make me feel more relaxed?"
- "What can I tell the interviewer to demonstrate the value that I can bring to the position?"

When you focus your attention on these kinds of questions, you will attract other similar thoughts. The only difference is that they will empower you rather than disempower you.

Reframe Worry as an Opportunity: Reframing is a method by which you can change your perspective of a situation in a way that supports you. Overthinking can make us feel anxious, and our perspective of a situation will tend to be negative when we are anxious. Further, we often believe that our perspective reflects reality.

As a result, we may not consider other perspectives that would benefit us. When reframing a situation, we create a shift in our mindset that allows us to see alternative perspectives. By seeing a situation from a different perspective, you can create a new meaning for a situation.

The following are simple steps that you can take use reframing. When doing this exercise, you should write down your answers.

1. Describe a situation that is bothering you.

    Example: I did not complete a project successfully for my supervisor.

2. Describe how the situation makes you feel.

    Example: I feel like I am incompetent.

3. Identify the negative thoughts that you are having about the situation.

    Example: I cannot do anything right.

4. Find evidence to support your negative thinking.

    Example: I did not complete the project.

5. Find evidence that does not support your negative thinking.

    Example: There are many times in the past when I did a good job.

6. Adopt more realistic thinking.

    Example: I made a mistake, but I can learn from it and get better.

7. Reevaluate your feelings after taking these steps.

    Example: I feel more compassionate toward myself, and I am eager to improve.

Use of Your Voice and Writing: It is easier to gain clarity in your thinking if you externalize your thoughts. Externalizing your thoughts means bringing them out of your head and into the open.

You can do that by sharing your thoughts with others or by writing about them.

Talking About It: Talking about your concerns is another way to relieve worries. When you talk about your concerns, they are no longer internalized. You are putting your concerns out into the open where you can better understand and process them. It is for this reason that having a strong support system is important for maintaining mental well-being. Find someone who you can talk to, be it a friend or a therapist.

If your concerns have to do with another person, talk to that person and express your concerns. Whether you like what their response is or not, it will provide you with a sense of relief or closure as you will no longer be internalizing your concerns.

Affirmations: Affirmations have the power to rewire our brains and develop new beliefs about ourselves. To be effective, affirmations need to be worded in an empowering way and resonate with you. The key to success with affirmations is to say them with emotion and conviction. When you do this, your affirmation becomes a focal point for your attention. It is by making your affirmation the focal point of your attention that changes in beliefs occur.

Each time you recite your affirmation, you strengthen the belief that your affirmation is true. It is this process that creates changes in beliefs. When you first start using affirmations, you may not notice any changes, but stay with it. You should start noticing changes after 30 days. What you may notice is that your old beliefs may appear, but they will be canceled out by your new way of thinking. The following are examples of affirmations:

- I deserve all the good things that come to me.
- I take time for self-care because I am worth it.
- I honor myself by being true to who I am.
- I honor and believe in myself.

Singing, Humming, and Chanting: The act of singing, humming, and chanting stimulates the body's system for recovering from stress. This relaxation response soothes the nervous system and brings the mind and body back to balance.

Laughing: The adage that laughter is the best medicine has a lot of truth to it. Laughing reduces stress by increasing the amount of oxygen in the body, which activates the body's relaxation response.

Journaling: Journaling is a great way for you to release your emotions and reflect on what you are experiencing. Make journaling part of your daily routine. You will gain insight into yourself and purge your mind of your excessive thinking.

Taking Charge of Your Focus: The problem is not that we experience negative thoughts or anxiety. The problem is that these things become the object of our attention. We experience what we focus on. If you experience a negative thought or anxiety, acknowledge it and then shift your focus to what you want to happen. You can do this using the following techniques:

Healthy Distractions: As humans, we are a gifted species in that we can be intentional about what we focus on. The challenge is that we may get caught up in overthinking and forget that we have this power. You have the power to shift your focus from thoughts and feelings that make you feel disempowered to focusing on things that empower you. This shift that is being described is what healthy distraction is all about.

We may engage in unhealthy distractions as a way to avoid experiencing feelings that we find unpleasant. An example of this is safety behaviors, which were previously described. When using unhealthy forms of distraction, we avoid unpleasant feelings but never address the problem.

Healthy distractions provide temporary relief from the problem until you are ready to deal with the situation. An example of this would be you find yourself getting upset with your partner. To avoid saying things that you may later regret, you decided to go for a walk. You then discuss the issue with your partner when you feel more in control of your emotions.

The following are examples of healthy distraction behaviors:

- Engage in exercise or physical activity.
- Listen to music.
- Read a book.
- Write in your journal.
- Have a healthy meal.
- Drink herbal tea.
- Watch a movie.
- Play video games.
- Meditate.
- Practice mindfulness.

- Express your creativity.
- Do housework.

Unhealthy distractions would be using coping strategies as a way to avoid feeling your emotions, which is known as self-medicating. Examples of this would be using drugs or alcohol. Unhealthy distractions may help you avoid strong feelings in the short term, but they do nothing to address the situation that is causing you suffering. Further, they often lead to other problems.

Create a New Perspective: Thoughts and feelings are the same energies but manifest in different ways. Your thoughts are experienced as the voice in your head while feelings are experienced as moods. Further, your thoughts and feelings will mirror each other. If you have negative thoughts, you will experience negative feelings. If you have positive feelings, you will have positive thoughts.

What determines whether these energies are experienced as being positive or negative is our perspective. Your perspective is your interpretation of a situation. Two people may lose their jobs. The first person may see their situation from a negative perspective. They may become anxious or depressed. The second person may see their situation as an opportunity to start their own business.

The only difference between these two people is that they had different perspectives of their situation. What determines our perspective is how we evaluate the situation, namely what the situation means to us. If you change the meaning that you give to a situation, you will change your perspective.

An effective way of changing the meaning that you give to a situation is through mindfulness. When practicing mindfulness, one learns to be an observer of that which they are experiencing rather than judging or personalizing it. A metaphor for this approach would be going birdwatching.

In birdwatching, one observes the bird and tries to gain information about it. At the same time, one takes care not to disturb the bird. If one is being mindful of a situation, one observes the situation without making it personal or judging it. By doing this, one gains new insights that may have been overlooked due to personalizing or judging it. In Chapter 4, you will find more detailed information about mindfulness. For now, here is a simple exercise that you can do to become mindful of your thoughts and behaviors:

1. Take a moment to become still. Try to avoid making judgments about anything you experience, including your thoughts and feelings. Do not make any effort to achieve or accomplish anything.
2. Be present with what you are experiencing. Notice what you are thinking, feeling, or doing.
3. As you remain present, gather information about what you are experiencing. Did you gain any insights from doing this? Did you develop a new perspective?

Inspire Your Senses: If you had trouble doing the previous technique, simplify it by finding things that inspire you. This could be as simple as watching a sunset, listening to your favorite music, or recalling a special memory. Whatever it is that inspires you, make that your point of focus.

In our technology-oriented society, it is easy to get addicted to our cellphones and other devices. This kind of behavior can make it difficult for personal reflection or to get in touch with how we experience sensory information. For this reason, it is advisable that you take breaks from your electronic devices and take time to experience how you respond to the non-digital world. This can be achieved by doing something as simple as taking a walk outside.

Sensory Experience: You can dissolve stress in an instant if you shift your attention from your thoughts to your sensory experience. The key is to find which sense works best for you. Is it seeing, hearing, tasting, smelling, or touching? To determine this, experiment with your different senses. The following are examples of how to use your five senses to direct your focus:

Seeing:

- Look at a photograph or other sentimental memento.
- Adorn your workspace with plants and flowers.
- Spend time in nature, be it your backyard or the mountains.
- Decorate your living space and workspace with colors.
- Visualize in your mind a place that you find relaxing.

Smelling:

- Burn scented candles or incense.
- Experiment using essential oils.
- Keep scented flowers in your space.
- Take in the odors of the outdoors.
- Wear cologne or perfume that you enjoy.

Touching:

- Snuggle with your partner.
- Get cozy by wrapping yourself in a blanket.
- Pet your dog or cat.
- Massage your hands or neck.
- Wear clothes that feel good against your skin.

Tasting:

- Savor your favorite foods.
- Sip herbal tea.
- Keep with you a favorite snack.
- Eat foods whose textures you enjoy.

Hearing:

- Listen to your favorite music.
- Listen to nature sound recordings.
- Get a small fountain for your workspace so that you can listen to the sound of running water.
- Spend time in nature so that you can listen to birds singing.

5-4-3-2-1 Method: The 5-4-3-2-1 method is similar to the previous technique; sensory experience. The only difference is that it is more systematic. To do this technique, focus on five things that you can see, four things that you can touch, three things that you can hear, two things that you can smell, and one thing that you can taste. Doing this will ground you and bring you into the present moment.

Practice Segmentation: Segmentation is a stress management technique where you designate a specific time to focus on the different areas of your life. Many of us deal with competing concerns that prevent us from focusing on any one thing. For example, you may be at work but your attention is on a family issue. When this happens, you are unable to give your best performance to your work, nor can you do much for your family.

Using segmentation, you learn to focus on what is happening at the moment. When you are at work, you focus on work. When you are at home, you focus on your family. If you are relaxing, your focus is on relaxing. In this manner, segmentation is practicing being present. When using segmentation, it is helpful to have transition periods. For example, upon leaving work and before arriving home, you can spend a few moments doing deep breathing exercises so that you can greet your family with a refreshed mind.

Practice Being Present: Practicing mindfulness is all about the recognition of the present moment; the now. Overthinking is often a fear-based response to what may happen in the future. We may believe that a negative situation is looming in our future and that we need to dwell in our thinking of all the ways that it may manifest.

The deeper truth is that time is an illusion and that the past and future are expressions of this illusion. Our experience of the past exists as a memory while our anticipations create the future. Both memory and anticipation are forms of thought, and these thoughts can only exist in the present moment.

Overthinking cannot occur if one's attention is on the present moment. When you are focused on the present moment, neither overthinking nor anxiety can exist. Both overthinking and anxiety exist because our focus is on what may happen in the future or what happened in the past.

There are times when it is useful to think about the future and past, such as when we want to reflect on how we can improve ourselves or when planning is needed. However, there needs to be a balance with a focus on the present moment. Chapter 4 will cover mindfulness in greater detail and techniques for becoming present, but here are things that you can do now to become more present:

- Cut Down on Your Device Time: In our technological age, cellphones and laptops are an integral part of our lives. While we may depend on them to do our jobs, many of us spend a lot of time scrolling and texting for nonessential reasons. These devices distract us from the present moment, and we lose our connection with the non-digital world. Instead of staring at a screen, focus on your immediate environment. Notice the sky, nature's creations, or the people around you. When you allow yourself to focus on the natural world, you will gain clarity about yourself and your world.

- Offer Your Full Attention to Others: This topic is related to the previous one. Because many of us have become addicted to our cellphones, our attention span has become worse. It has come to the point that our cellphones often receive more of our attention than the people around us, including those whom we love and care for. When engaging with others, give the other person your full attention. A trick that I have used is to tell myself that the next words someone says to me will be the most important words I will ever hear.

- Multitasking - It Is a Myth: In the recent past, multitasking has become a catchphrase that has been promoted, especially by the business community. However, the benefit of multitasking is largely a myth. It poses risks to our emotional and physical well-being.

  To begin with, most research shows that the quality of performance improves when we do one task at a time. Multitasking not only compromises our ability to concentrate but it can lead to increased stress and less efficiency. More importantly, it takes us out of the present moment.

- Give Yourself a Break: Compared to many other countries, Americans spend more time working. We often work through our breaks, and we often do not use our vacation time. It is hard to be present when we are always pushing ourselves. What we do get from pushing ourselves is burnout and decreased life satisfaction. It is important throughout the day to take breaks and to schedule time off for yourself.

- Be With Your Emotions: Next time you experience negative emotions, try to be with them instead of getting caught up in them. When we experience a negative emotion, we often get caught up in the feelings we experience. This can cause us to be reactive and do things that we will later regret. Try being with your emotions instead.

  When you experience a negative emotion, allow yourself to experience it but focus on what is in your environment. By focusing on your environment, you will ground yourself in it, which will keep you from getting caught up in your emotions.

Simultaneously, you are not denying your emotions as you are allowing yourself to experience them.

- Focus on Your Breath: Focusing on your breath will instantly ground you in the present moment. The reason for this is that you are diverting your attention from your thoughts to your breath, which has a calming effect. Also, focusing on your breath will cause you to breathe deeper, which will further enhance feelings of calm.

Using the Body: The mind and body are one. Our mind affects the body, and the body affects the mind. Though we may believe that thinking occurs in the mind, the truth is that the body has an intelligence of its own. The mind and body are continuously exchanging information with each other to keep us functioning. The following are techniques utilizing the power of your body to calm your mind:

1. **Trust Your Gut Instincts:** We tend to put greater trust in logic and rational thinking than in our gut feelings. However, doing so downplays a valuable tool that we have at our disposal. Our gut instincts, or intuition, have served us for thousands of years. When making a decision, our brains use both logic and emotions. Our decision-making is also influenced by biases and faulty thinking.

    Your gut instinct is the culmination of countless past experiences where your brain processed sensory information. That information allows us to make predictions based on what happened in the past. This whole process occurs subconsciously so we are not aware of it. An example of this is when you are driving, and you have something on your mind. Suddenly, you have the thought that you need to slow down, which saves you from getting into an accident. That thought that you needed to slow down was based on your gut feeling. You can learn to trust your gut feelings by doing the following:

- Pay Attention to Your First Thoughts About a Situation: It is important to notice what your first thought is when you meet someone or enter a situation. Notice what your first reaction is. That first thought will be an important data point when you make a decision.
- Determine if Bias Is a Factor: It is important to investigate whether that first thought is your gut instinct or a psychological bias. One way to determine this is by the existence or absence of an emotional reaction. If your first thought results in you experiencing an emotional reaction, your thought may be based on a psychological bias.
  A psychological bias refers to when we unconsciously make an irrational decision. An example of a psychological bias would be looking only for evidence that supports your viewpoint. If the first thought is not accompanied by an emotional reaction, it is most likely your gut instinct sending you a message.
- Fine-Tune Your Gut Instincts: You can learn to fine-tune your gut instincts through practice. You can do this by paying attention to your body and what you are experiencing in certain situations. For example, if you are meeting someone for the first time, what do you experience in your body? What is it telling you? Did what you experience turn out to be true

about the other person? Follow this procedure over some time so that you can stack up your experiences.

Each time, check to see if your gut feeling was correct or not. I recommend that you keep score of the times you were right and wrong. Over time, you will have a decent sample size to determine your accuracy. By paying close attention to what you are experiencing, you will be able to distinguish between your gut intuition and psychological biases.

You can also challenge the validity of your gut instincts by asking yourself the following questions:

How Much Experience Do I Have Regarding My Current Situation: Your gut instinct evolves with time and experience. The more experience you have in a given area, the greater your gut instinct will be. A veteran police officer will have a stronger gut instinct for their job than a new recruit will.

How Predictable Is This Environment: The ability to make predictions comes from having experienced similar situations in the past, so you recognize certain patterns. For example, if you have gone to restaurants before, you recognize that there are certain patterns that you can expect. The host will show you to your table, and the waiter will follow to take your order. If it is your first time at a restaurant, you will not know what to expect. How fast do I need to decide on the situation? When you are in a high-pressure situation, where you cannot wait on deciding, it is best to go by your gut instincts as it is the only resource for deciding what you have.

Am I Being Influenced by My Psychological Biases: The only thing that you can do for this step is to do some self-reflection.

You will need to get honest with yourself and determine if you are open to considering information that may not be consistent with any psychological biases that you may have. An example of this would be admitting to yourself that you decided out of peer pressure rather than by what you truly believe.

2. Focus on Your Heartbeat: Focusing on your heartbeat brings about a sense of calmness and a feeling of wholeness. You can more easily feel your heartbeat by placing your hand on your heart.

3. Eye Movement: A quick way to reduce stress is through eye movement. While keeping your head still, move your eyes side to side between two predetermined points. Repeat this twenty-five times. For the two predetermined points, you can place your hands on your knees or use the two sides of a piece of furniture.

4. Get Plenty of Sleep: A lack of adequate sleep can lead to increased anxiety and negative thinking. Try getting 7-8 hours of sleep. You will find that you will be better able to handle anxiety and stress. It should be noted that overthinking can cause problems getting to sleep. By trying the other techniques mentioned in this section, in a particular exercise, you should find it easier to fall asleep.

5. Physical Movement: As stated in the previous section, the body has an intelligence of its own. Tapping into that intelligence can calm your mind and provide clarity in thinking. Accessing that intelligence may sometimes require your body to be in motion. The following are techniques for using physical movement to positively impact your mind:

- Exercise: Exercise is another effective way to break the anxiety cycle. Exercising provides a healthy distraction from worrisome thoughts. Additionally, exercise causes the release of endorphins; a hormone that brings about feelings of happiness.

  The best exercises for the release of endorphins are aerobic exercises, such as jogging, swimming, cycling, or any other exercise that gets your blood pumping.

- Power Moves and Power Poses: The mind and body are one. What happens to the mind shows up in the body. What happens in the body affects the mind. How you use your body can make you feel more powerful and confident, which is the purpose of power moves and power poses.

  Power moves are movements that make you feel powerful. An example of this is pumping your fist or walking confidently. Power poses involve adopting a position that makes you feel powerful. An example of this is taking a confident stance, placing your hands on your hips, puffing out your chest, and breathing deeply. By holding such a position for a few minutes, you may find yourself feeling more confident.

- Shaking: Stress and anxiety are the result of the nervous system becoming overstimulated. You can return your nervous system to balance by making shaking movements. You can do this by dancing, bouncing, or wiggling your body.

- Swing Your Arms: This simple exercise is part of my morning routine. It will limber you up and move your body's energy, which will make managing stress easier.

1. While standing straight, relax your neck and shoulders.

2. While remaining stationary, turn your waist from side to side so that your arms follow. The motion of your arms should result in them contacting your abdomen and lower back. Continue this motion for as long as you desire.

6. The Power of Touch: While physical movement can positively affect your mind, sometimes all that is needed is just the power of touch.

- Tapping: Tapping is similar to acupuncture, without needles. Instead, you use your fingers to tap on the body's meridian points. Tapping the meridian points disrupts the body's response to stress.

- Ear Massage: It is well-known that getting a massage can help relieve stress, but getting a massage is not practical in many situations, such as during a job interview. There is a massage; however, that you can do almost anywhere and at any time. The massage that is being referred to is an ear massage.

  There are pressure points in the ear that, when stimulated, can lead to positive health benefits, including anxiety and stress reduction. Use your forefinger and thumb to rub the top of your ear and then work downward along the edges. Doing this will increase blood flow and stimulate the nerve endings in your ear, resulting in you feeling more awake and alert.

- Touch the Earth: The earth balances the body's energy, but it needs to make contact with bare skin. By going barefoot, you will benefit from the earth's balancing forces. Spend time standing barefoot on sand or grass.

- Dip Your Wrist: Dip your wrist in cold water. Doing this will reduce stress symptoms such as cortisol levels and heart rate while increasing hormones that promote feeling good.

- Let Your Feet Roll: You can reduce stress by using a golf ball. Place a golf ball on the floor and step on it. While applying pressure, move your foot in a triangular motion. Doing this will relieve tension and anxiety.

7. Overcome Perfectionism: One of the causes of overthinking is perfectionism. Perfectionism is a personality trait that differs from being a high achiever. The motivation to be a higher achiever comes from wanting to do one's best. The motivation of a perfectionist is based on fear. Perfectionists generally have problems with self-esteem. Their self-esteem is based on their ability to do a task perfectly. Unless they can do the task perfectly, they feel that they may be judged.

This kind of mentality places a great deal of pressure on them. For this reason, people who are perfectionists often have a problem with procrastination. They feel that if they cannot do something perfectly, it is better to not do it at all. This puts them in a no-win situation because they set standards for themselves that they cannot achieve. If you have perfectionist tendencies, there are things that you can do to overcome them:

- Become Self-Aware: As with anything else in life, we need to become self-aware before we can make any kind of changes within ourselves. To become self-aware of your perfectionist tendencies, take time for self-reflection by identifying the thought patterns that drive you to achieve perfection. To do this, it is best to write down your thoughts as this will provide you with greater clarity. By becoming aware of your perfectionism thinking, you can then move on to make changes.

- Look for the Positive: Start paying attention to what you did right instead of what you perceive to be a mistake. Nothing in life will ever be perfect because we all are imperfect human beings. When you believe that you fell short on a project, balance it out by looking for something that you did right. When you come from a place where you desire to improve, you will get a lot further than if you come from a place where you fear making a mistake.

- Be Forgiving of Your Mistakes: Being accepting of your mistakes will provide you with the realization that your world will not end if you make one. More importantly, mistakes are a form of feedback that allows us to grow and improve.

- Set Realistic Goals: As previously mentioned, perfectionists tend to set unrealistic goals for themselves, which only invites failure. Instead, set realistic goals that you can achieve. Doing so will cause you less pressure while providing you with challenges that are motivating rather than fearful. To set realistic goals, you can use SMART goals. Refer back to

Chapter 2 for details on using SMART goals and other goal-setting techniques.

- Use Criticism as a Benefit: Each person brings their unique perspective to a given situation. For this reason, welcome constructive criticism. Constructive criticism provides insights that we may have missed because of our perspective. By learning from others' perspectives, our perspective expands.

- Stop Being Hard on Yourself: We tend to put more pressure on ourselves than anyone else. If you are a perfectionist, the amount of pressure that you put on yourself is even greater. There is only one standard that anyone can realistically live by, which is doing your best. Doing your best is attainable, being perfect is not.

- Put Meaning Over Perfection: Want to live a life where you feel fulfilled? Then find the meaning behind why you do what you do. You need to find an empowering meaning for anything that you do in life. The meaning that you get from doing something can be as simple as that it gives you enjoyment. Regardless of what something means to you, it will be more fulfilling than trying to be perfect. Again, trying to be perfect is a reactive response that is based on fear of not being good enough. Finding meaning will build your character and give you courage.

- Avoid Procrastination: As with animals, the human brain is designed to keep us from experiencing painful situations and to gravitate toward pleasurable ones. Those who are perfectionists distract themselves from feelings of insecurity by focusing on trying to get things perfect. However, their attempts to reach perfection are also painful, so they will often procrastinate.

In turn, procrastination reinforces their sense of low self-esteem. As a result, they find themselves in a vicious circle. Instead of procrastinating, adopt an attitude that you are not going to strive for perfection. Instead, ask yourself what it would mean to you to complete the project and do so to the best of your abilities. It can also help to break down the project into smaller steps and take one step at a time. For example, your first step may be to create an outline. By breaking down the task into smaller steps, you will create momentum.

- Guard Yourself Against Media Influences: The media is rich in content that will lead you to believe that you are not good enough; that you are missing out in life. This kind of content is particularly common in social media. Do not try to be like the latest social media influencer or what the ads portray. Such portrayals by the media only feed into perfectionist tendencies. Instead of trying to be like someone else, try to bring out the best of who you are.

- Consider Therapy: Seeing a therapist can be very helpful in overcoming perfectionism. A therapist can provide insights into your behavior that may take you a lot longer if you try doing it on your own. They can also support you. One particular form of therapy, cognitive behavioral therapy (CBT), is scientifically-based and has proven to be effective in treating perfectionism.

While the techniques in this book do work, many of them require practice before they will be effective in calming your mind. It is like a skilled martial artist. Such an individual can react in an instant to block a punch. However, they had to spend much time practicing before they could develop this ability. The same is true with any of these techniques.

When you find yourself in a stressful situation, you will most likely forget about these techniques and react to the situation through habit. However, if you practice these techniques enough times, you will develop a new habit. You will get to the point where you do not even have to think about using them. You will carry them out without even thinking about it.

To begin practicing, make the intention to practice using them throughout the course of your day. For example, if you are standing in line and begin to feel stressed, use your technique. By starting small, you can work up to more stressful situations.

8. Practicing Self-Care: Practicing self-care is an important aspect of managing anxiety, which in turn can help with overthinking. One cannot have a calm mind when one is focused on everything else but their well-being. By reading this book and applying its principles, you are engaging in self-care.

Additionally, anything else that you can do that will bring you a sense of peace and a feeling of health can be considered self-care. Regardless of what you do for self-care, you should make it a priority in your life. The decisions that you make in life are only as good as your ability to make them in an intentional rather than a reactive manner.

The Most Important Thing to Understand Is: A leading cause for overthinking is anxiety and throughout this book, you will find techniques for reducing anxiety. Many of these techniques involve distraction, the shifting of your attention from troubling thoughts or feelings and redirecting them toward something else.

While distracting yourself from anxiety can be a helpful tool in managing your anxiety, you should not depend on distraction techniques to deal with anxiety. Distraction techniques are useful for managing anxiety, but they do not address anxiety itself.

The most effective way of dealing with anxiety is to learn to accept it. There is a saying, "What we resist persists." This saying is particularly true when it comes to anxiety. If you try to resist your anxiety, it will persist as a problem for you. It is for this reason that distraction techniques should not be depended upon because distracting your attention is a form of resistance as it prevents you from learning to accept your anxiety.

The most effective way to deal with anxious feelings is to fully accept them into your life without any judgments about them or yourself. Instead of resisting your feelings of anxiety, try the following steps instead:

- Recognize the Presence of Your Anxiety: Tell yourself that the feeling of anxiety has appeared because you are worried about _____.
- Practice Nonjudgment: Do not judge or criticize what you are experiencing or yourself. Tell yourself that your body is responding to your thoughts of concern for your situation. Also, tell yourself that it is okay to feel this way.

- Acknowledge Your Power: Anxiety cannot control you unless you allow it to. By accepting your anxiety instead of reacting to it, you can continue to function despite it.

There were times in the past when you felt anxious but pushed through with what you had to do despite it. You were able to do so because you became intentional. You told yourself you had to handle the situation. By learning to accept your anxious feeling, you can continue to live your life as you will be in charge. In Chapter 4, you will learn about how to use mindfulness to get to know your anxiety, rather than reacting to it.

9. When to Seek Help: There are times when using the techniques in this book is not sufficient for dealing with anxiety. For some of us, seeing a therapist may be needed. Signs that your anxiety may require the attention of a professional include:

- Your anxiety is pervasive in that you feel it almost all the time.
- Your anxiety interferes with your personal or work life.
- You experience panic attacks.

Check with your health insurance provider for authorized mental health providers. Normally, it takes 8 to 10 sessions of cognitive behavioral therapy (CBT) to regain control of anxiety disorders (Glen, 2014).

In the next chapter, we will explore other ways to bring about a more peaceful mind. Through the use of meditation and mindfulness, you can bring about positive change by going deeper within.

Chapter 4:
Essential Relaxation Techniques - From A(nxious) to Z(en)

"Worry pretends to be necessary but serves no useful purpose." ~
Eckhart Tolle

When I was younger, I used to be a chronic worrier. However, I did not see that as a problem. I honestly thought worrying was a good thing. I believed that worrying made me better prepared to deal with potential problems that may arise in the future. I believed that to not worry was to leave myself open to potential threats.

I now understand how dysfunctional my thinking was at the time. Preparing yourself for potential problems is being responsible. Worrying about problems and not taking any action to deal with them is just a waste of mental energy. Worrying serves no purpose. Despite this fact, many of us continue to worry, which leads to overthinking.

There is a story about a man who was walking down a road. The man sees a rider on a horse approaching him. The man could see that the rider was struggling to hold on as his horse ran uncontrollably toward the man. When the rider got close enough, the man asked him where he was going in such a rush. The rider responded by saying, "I do not know, ask the horse."

The horse is a metaphor for our minds when we overthink. We have no control over it; it has control over us. However, there is a way that we can regain control of our minds so that we are in charge. The practice of mindfulness is one way of doing so. Mindfulness is an ancient practice of developing one's awareness of the present moment. The present moment encompasses everything that we experience, both within us and around us. By becoming mindful, we can avoid the pitfalls of overthinking.

When practicing mindfulness, one is not thinking about what may happen in the future, nor is one thinking about what happened in the past. Being mindful is being aware of what is happening in the present moment. When one is focused on the present moment, there is no judgment. Because one is not thinking about the past, there is no regret or sorrow. Because one is not thinking about the future, there is no worry or anticipation.

You may think that becoming mindful is a tall order that requires much training and discipline. In truth, being mindful requires no effort. What does take effort is overthinking. Because we are so used to it, we do it effortlessly. However, do not be deceived by this. Overthinking requires a tremendous amount of mental energy, which is often why we feel mentally tired.

Being mindful, on the other hand, just requires us to BE. When I say that we just need to BE, I am referring to being in our natural state where our attention is on the present moment without any judgment. Further, we all have experienced this, though perhaps for only brief moments.

Consider the following examples of being in the present moment:
- You were looking in awe at the beauty of the natural world, such as a spectacular sunset or a natural landscape.

- You held your newborn baby for the first time.
- You were in a deep state of relaxation.
- You were spending time with someone who you were in love with.
- Those brief moments when you first wake up when you are free of thoughts.

These examples demonstrate that we have moments of mindfulness even when we do not intend it. By approaching mindfulness intentionally, you can experience mindfulness most of the time rather than just during those rare occasions. The following are exercises that you can do to cultivate mindfulness to help reduce overthinking:

The Awareness Diary: To be mindful is to be aware of what is happening both within and outside you. So, being mindful is to be aware of the thoughts that you are having, the emotions that they are triggering, and how those emotions are being experienced in the body. By developing this degree of awareness, you can stop overthinking before it leads to anxiety or stress. Just as importantly, you can then use mindfulness to bring calmness and reset.

Keeping an awareness diary will allow you to track your thoughts, emotions, and bodily experiences. For one week, notate the following in your awareness diary:

- Your ongoing thoughts that you are experiencing
- The emotions that you are experiencing while having those thoughts
- How you experience these emotions in your body

After a week, review your diary and see if you can identify patterns in your thoughts, emotions, and bodily sensations. By identifying your patterns, you will know how to respond so that you do not get caught up in them.

Question Your Thinking: As mentioned earlier, our emotions reflect our thoughts. Thoughts will lead to emotions that are of like kind. If you are experiencing unpleasant emotions, it is because you are having unpleasant thoughts. When you are experiencing unpleasant emotions, identify the thoughts that are creating them. When you have identified the thoughts, challenge them by asking yourself questions like these:

- What is causing me to have these thoughts? What is the underlying fear in these thoughts?

- Do these thoughts reflect the reality of the situation or am I making the situation worse than it has to be?

- Are there more empowering thoughts that I could be having about the situation? What would happen if I chose to hold on to those thoughts instead?

By challenging your thinking, you may come to realize that your thoughts were blowing things out of proportion and that you would be better served by adopting more empowering thinking.
Learn to Appreciate the Unknown: As humans, we tend to seek certainty. Many feel anxious when there is uncertainty. There is a part of us that finds uncertainty as being threatening. We want to know that we can count on something, that there is something that we can depend on. However, the human condition is a paradox as we have conflicting needs. We need to have both certainty and uncertainty in

our lives. If we only had certainty in our lives, there would be no need to challenge ourselves nor would we grow.

Uncertainty is the realm of unlimited possibilities while certainty is restrictive. If we are certain about something, we will not consider other possibilities. I remember a time when I was having trouble with my car. I was so sure that I knew what the problem was. I also knew that getting it repaired would be expensive. As I waited for my scheduled time with my mechanic, I spent a lot of time worrying about how I was going to fit the needed repairs into my budget.

When I brought my car to the mechanic, I received a pleasant surprise. My mechanic informed me that the problem with my car was not what I thought. Further, it would be a minor repair, which I could afford. In this case, my sense of certainty caused me emotional upset. If I had opened up myself to being uncertain about my car problems, I would have probably not worried so much.

You learn to be more accepting of uncertainty by becoming more mindful in your daily life. This can be accomplished by avoiding making judgments about the situations that you encounter. When you find yourself in an uncertain situation, do not judge it and make it into something negative. Instead, accept the fact that the situation is uncertain and focus on the different opportunities that the situation can provide.

I once lost my job as a teacher, and I was having difficulty finding a new job. Though I sent out plenty of resumes, I was getting no response. I was getting concerned because our savings were getting low. During one of my morning meditations, I experienced a shift in my mind. A feeling came over me that told me everything would be okay.

The result of that experience was that I started to approach my job search with a sense of confidence. Sure enough, I found out about a job opening at a university for a position that I never heard of before. I applied for the position and got hired on the same day that I interviewed. Learn to give up your need for certainty while becoming more appreciative of uncertainty.

Learn to Meditate: In my opinion, one of the most powerful things that you can do to empower your life is to learn to meditate. One of the major benefits of practicing meditation is the level of mindfulness that you can achieve. When we are not mindful, we personalize or identify with our thoughts and emotions. What I mean by this is that we allow our thoughts and emotions to define who we are.

As you learn to meditate, there will be a point when you realize that who you are, at the deepest level, is not your thoughts and emotions. Rather, you are the one who is aware of these things.

When you reach this point of realization, negative thoughts and emotions will not disturb you. They will simply be a part of your experience. You can remain in a calm space despite their presence. It is like the cloud and the sky. You are the sky while your thoughts and emotions are clouds. Clouds transverse the sky, but the sky remains undisturbed by them.

Similarly, thoughts and emotions can transverse the vastness of your awareness, but you will remain undisturbed by them. You can make learning to meditate easier by observing the following guidelines:

- Do not have any expectations of what should be happening when meditating. Whatever it is that you experience, allow it to happen.

- Meditation does not mean you are free of thoughts. Many people experience racing thoughts when trying to meditate. Do not try to resist your thoughts. Accept the fact that you are having thoughts and allow them to come and go on their own accord.

- While meditating, do not judge anything that you experience.

- It takes practice to learn how to meditate. Practice for a few minutes each day; however, try to increase the time that you practice each day.

- When meditating, there is nothing for you to do other than to be aware of what you are experiencing.

The Four-Step Pause: The Four-Step Pause is a mindfulness exercise for reminding you of your self-care needs. When doing this exercise, it is best to do it in a place where you feel comfortable and will not be disturbed. Next time you find yourself stressed out from overthinking, do the following:

1. Spend some time listening to the sounds in your environment. To do this focus on each sound individually. As you focus on the sound, notice how it comes in and out of your awareness.

2. Next, place your attention on the bodily sensations caused by your body making contact with the environment. Some examples of this would be the sensation of your feet touching

the floor, where your body makes contact with the chair or the weight of your hands on your lap.

3. Take a couple of deep breaths and notice the air flowing into your body and toward your belly. If it is helpful, you can count your breaths. Continue this step until you feel your body becoming relaxed.

4. When you are feeling relaxed, ask yourself, "What do I need to do to take care of myself?" Remain silent until you receive a response. The response that you receive may be as simple as that you need to take a break or go for a walk. Whatever it is, follow through by doing it.

Sitting in Discomfort: It is natural to want to avoid experiencing feelings. Though this is a normal reaction, that does not mean it is the best way to deal with discomfort. Discomfort is a feeling that we experience. However, feelings are just energies that are created by the body.

We may say that happiness is a good feeling while fear is a bad one. However, "good" and "bad" are just labels that our minds create, which we use to identify the feeling. These energies are neither good nor bad; they are just energies. By learning to experience your feelings with mindfulness, you can learn to accept any feeling that you are having without judgment.

Next time you experience feelings of discomfort, do not try to avoid or change them. Accept them as being part of the body's energy field. Take some time to be with them; do so without any judgment. Treat your feelings of discomfort as a small child who wants to be acknowledged and listened to. Remain silent and try to understand what your feelings are trying to communicate to you. The more you can sit with your feelings, the less of an impact they will have on you. When this happens, you will experience a calmer mind.

Mindfulness for Bedtime: Many of us experience overthinking at bedtime, making it difficult to fall asleep. Practicing mindfulness can help slow down your mind so that you can sleep better. However, before getting into mindfulness exercises, it is worth noting that there are certain activities that you should not engage in before going to bed, as they can contribute to having difficulty sleeping:

- Your bed should be for sleeping, not reading or watching television. If you reserve your bed for sleeping, you will condition your mind and body to associate your bed with sleeping.

- This has already been stated, but it deserves repeating. Do not look at your cellphone when in bed. The light from these gadgets will lower your melatonin levels, making it difficult to sleep.

- If you have trouble sleeping, go to another room to read, meditate, or do breathing exercises. When you are feeling more relaxed, return to bed.

The following exercises will help you become more mindful. Though they are great for relaxing before going to bed, you can do them anytime you want to calm your mind.

The Body Scan: The body scan is a simple exercise where you place the focus of your attention on the sensations of the body. By focusing on your bodily sensations, you are diverting your attention from your thoughts. This exercise can be done while sitting in a chair or lying on the floor.

1. Take a deep breath, hold it, and slowly exhale. Let the air out in a controlled fashion.
2. Now breathe normally. As you breathe, place your attention on your breath. Notice the sensations you experience as your breath travels in and out of your body.
3. Place your attention on the sensations in your feet.
4. Next, place your attention on your legs. Notice the sensations that you experience in your legs.
5. Now place your attention on your hips and buttocks. Notice the sensations that you experience in these areas.
6. Now focus on your upper torso, which includes your stomach, chest, and back. Notice the sensations that you experience in your upper torso.
7. Focus on your shoulders and arms. Notice the sensations that you experience in your shoulders and arms.
8. Focus on your hands. Notice the sensations that you experience in your hands.
9. Place your attention on your face. Notice the sensations that you experience in this area.
10. Now take a deep breath, hold it, and slowly exhale.
11. Feel your entire body becoming relaxed. Immerse yourself in the sense of relaxation that is in your body.

Yoga: Doing yoga is another effective way to calm your mind and promote well-being. Yoga has been shown to regulate the body's stress response and reduce stress. With the reduction of stress comes a decrease in anxiety levels. Additionally, the stretching involved in yoga releases muscle tension, which further enhances the mind's relaxation.

Breathing Exercises: Chapter 3 discussed the anxiety cycle. When we get caught in a cycle of worrying, it breeds anxiety. However, there is another element that plays a key role in this cycle, and that element is the breath.

When we worry or overthink, we are diverting our attention from our breathing and giving it to our thoughts. Because we are not being mindful of our breathing, we may develop bad breathing habits. Probably the most common bad breathing habit is shallow breathing.

When we do not breathe fully, we are not optimizing the amount of oxygen that we take into the body. With less oxygen, we can become anxious, which in turn can lead to overthinking. Overthinking then maintains shallow breathing.

When we breathe fully, we increase the amount of oxygen that is introduced into the body while expelling a greater amount of carbon dioxide. When this occurs, the body gets into a relaxed state. In turn, the mind also relaxes.

Grounding Techniques: Grounding techniques are used to return us to the present moment. By doing so, our attention is removed from our anxious feelings or overthinking. The following are examples of such techniques:

1. **Physical Grounding Techniques:** Physical grounding techniques involve the use of the five senses to reduce anxiety.

   - Focus on Objects: Select an object that is near you and focus on its texture, weight, and color. Is its texture smooth or rough? Is it heavy or light? What color is it? The more detailed your focus is on the object, the more you will create a distance between yourself and overthinking.

   - Eat and Drink Mindfully: When eating, we often spend more time focusing on our thoughts than on what we are eating or drinking. Reverse this by focusing on what you are consuming. Savor your food and drink. When eating, focus on the smell, taste, and texture of your food before you swallow it. Do the same with what you are drinking.

   - Take in the Odor: Besides savoring the aroma of food, focus on the odor of other things like soap or candles.

   - Tune Into Your Body: Take time to focus on how your body feels. By directing your attention to different parts of your body, you will ground yourself in your body as opposed to your mind. Examples of this include:
     - Focus on what your hair feels like on your body.
     - Feel the weight of your clothing on your body.
     - Feel the sensations of your heart beating.
     - Notice if your arms are loose or stiff.
     - Notice if your shoulders are tight or relaxed.

- How do your feet feel in your shoes or what are the sensations as you walk?

2. **Mental Grounding Techniques:** Mental grounding techniques work by distracting us mentally from our thoughts, thus bringing us into the present.

    - Create a Memory Challenge: Look at a detailed picture or photograph and study it for about ten seconds. Look away from the image and try to recall everything you saw.

    - Break Down Categories: Think of a general category and then mentally list all the items that would belong to that category. Example: If your category is Italian food, think of all the Italian dishes that you can think of.

    - Focus on Numbers: Make your knowledge of numbers the focus of your attention. The following are examples:
        - Count from 100 backward.
        - Mentally go through the multiplication table.
        - Think about five different ways that you can arrive at a number. Example: If your number is six, think of five different ways that you can use addition, subtraction, multiplication, and division to achieve that number.

    - Recitation: Recite to yourself a song, poem, or passage from a book.

- Describe Your Surroundings: Take a few minutes to describe to yourself what your surroundings are like. When describing your surroundings, incorporate all your senses and get as detailed as you can. Example: "The coffee shop that I am sitting in is empty. I can smell the aroma of coffee. Through the window, I can see trees whose leaves are moving with the wind. There is mellow music coming from the speakers, and the chair that I am sitting in feels comfortable."

3. Grounding Techniques That Soothe: These techniques can be used to promote soothing feelings and can be used to cancel out or lower the intensity of negative feelings.

    - Carry Your Loved Ones in Your Mind: If you are experiencing an emotional upset, try to imagine the face of a loved one or what they sound like. You can imagine them telling you to not give up and that they will always be there for you.

    - Seek Comfort From Your Pet: If you have a pet, spend time with them. If you have a cat or dog, pay attention to what it feels like as you pet them. Also, pay attention to their physical appearance and habits. You can also hold your pet and pay attention to what that feels like. If you are away from your pet, think about what it would be like to have them with you.

    - Try Lavender Oil: Lavender oil induces calmness and can help with sleep issues and headaches as well. Keep a bottle of lavender oil near you and take a sniff or apply some to your temples when you are feeling anxious.

- Visit Your Favorite Spot: If possible, go to your favorite place and spend time there. If that is not possible, take an imaginary trip there by visualizing it in your mind. When you visualize your favorite place, include details of what you would see, hear, smell, taste, and touch.

- Touch Your Comfort Item: Touch something that feels good to you, such as a blanket, well-worn jeans, or a soft t-shirt. If you do not have these things with you, imagine what they would feel like.

- Listen to Good Music: Music can have a powerful effect on how we feel. Listen to songs that you find comforting. Also, when listening to your songs, listen to them as though you are hearing them for the first time.

In the next chapter, we will discuss what happens when we have difficulty making a decision.

The Power of Shared Experiences

For many who wrestle with the ceaseless gears of overthinking, finding a voice that resonates can be like finding a guiding star on a cloudy night. The restless nights, the spirals of rumination, the constant "what ifs" ... It is an exhausting, oftentimes lonesome road. And while the journey to inner peace is personal, the struggles along the way are shared by countless others.

Before you discovered the tools and strategies laid out in this book, perhaps you felt adrift in an ocean of your own thoughts. Maybe you felt unique in your struggles, burdened with a challenge that seemed incomprehensible to others. However, the truth is far from it. Countless souls are trapped in the whirlwind of overanalysis, seeking an escape or a beacon of understanding.

My aspiration in crafting this book was two-fold: to offer you a compass to navigate the stormy seas of overthinking and to assure you that your vessel is not solitary in these vast waters. And here is where you can do something profound – extend a lifeline to another.

By dedicating a few minutes to pen a review on Amazon, you are not just reflecting on your own journey but illuminating the path for others. Your honest insights provide a beacon for others lost in the tempest of their own thoughts, showcasing that there is a community, a guiding light, and most importantly, hope.

Your reflections about the strategies that resonated with you, the chapters that became your go-to, or even the areas you felt could have delved deeper into – all of them contribute to a rich tapestry of experiences. This tapestry not only represents your journey but also offers a glimpse to others about what awaits them.

Scan to leave a review

In essence, your words could be the nudge someone needs to start their journey toward finding inner peace. It could be the validation another seeks, assuring them that they are not alone in their battles. So, while I am genuinely grateful for your feedback, be it positive or constructive, it is truly the countless others yet to embark on this journey who stand to benefit the most from your shared wisdom.

Thank you for being a part of this shared voyage. Together, we are not just battling overthinking; we are building bridges of understanding and solidarity.

Chapter 5:
Analysis Paralysis: Evacuation Plan

"If you spend too much time thinking about a thing, you will never get it done." ~ Bruce Lee

Do you ever find yourself having difficulty making decisions? Well, you are not alone. We live in an information-based society where we are confronted with more information than at any other time in human history. With more information available to us comes more options to choose from.

For those of us who are overthinkers, the challenge of making a decision is further magnified. Consider the fact that the average person makes an estimated 35,000 decisions each day. There are times when we need to spend time making thoughtful decisions, such as when the outcome of our decisions may make a major impact on our lives. However, what if our difficulty in making a decision extends to areas that are not life-altering? If you experience this, you may have an analysis of paralysis.

What Is Analysis Paralysis?

Put simply, analysis paralysis is overthinking a problem to the point that you are unable to make a decision. Analysis paralysis does not only affect individuals; it can also affect groups and organizations. Analysis paralysis often occurs when we have multiple options to choose from, which appear to be equally viable. It can also occur when your options are too broad or too vague. To illustrate this, let us use the example of a business owner. They have a choice of either increasing their profits or expanding their customer outreach. In this case, both options seem equally viable. Now, consider this: The business owner is trying to decide where they should advertise. In this case, their research parameters are too broad or vague.

Instead of asking the question, "Where should I advertise," they could ask the question, "Where should I advertise, that will result in the greatest interest?" This more specific research parameter can make decision-making easier. These same principles apply to us as individuals. We are either feeling overwhelmed by our choices, or we have not clearly defined the question that we are asking ourselves.

What Kind of Decisions Most Often Lead to Analysis Paralysis?

The more impactful the decision we need to make, the more likely we will experience analysis paralysis. The reason for this is that such decisions have a greater impact on our well-being or the well-being of others. Such decisions include areas such as family, career, and finances. When trying to make decisions in these areas, it is easy for us to overthink or seek the opinions of too many people. In doing this, we end up with too much information, which makes decision-making difficult.

What Does Analysis Paralysis Feel Like?

When experiencing analysis paralysis, the feeling is not pleasant. You may experience stress, frustration, and racing thoughts. These things build up until you feel like you are too mentally drained to determine what to do. Additionally, you may experience stress-related symptoms such as:

- Anxiety
- Rapid heartbeat
- Ruminating thoughts
- Sweating
- Shallow breathing
- Fatigue
- Inability to sleep
- Avoiding decision making
- Less productivity
- Inability to focus
- Fear of failure
- Loss of confidence

Traits Associated With Analysis Paralysis

Anyone can experience analysis paralysis; however, certain personality traits are more susceptible to it:

All-or-Nothing Thinking: Those of us who have all-or-nothing thinking see things as being either good or bad. There are no gray areas or in between. When none of the options to choose from fit into one of these categories, analysis paralysis may occur.

Perfectionist Attitude: Having a perfectionist mindset can make decision-making more difficult. The ability to predict the outcome of our decisions, that involve areas of great impact, is often not possible. This can be difficult for perfectionists to accept. Further, those with perfectionist attitudes tend to have a fear of failure or disapproval. This fear creates added stress.

People Pleasers: Those with people-pleasing tendencies fear disappointing others. As a result, we tend to try to make others happy, even when it comes at our own expense. When the decision we need to make involves others, especially those whom we are close to, our people-pleasing mindset creates added pressure.

Lack of Confidence: There are several reasons why we may lack confidence when trying to make a decision. Some never developed decision-making skills, as others may have made most of their decisions for them. Others may have made bad decisions in the past and are afraid of repeating the past. Regardless of the reason, these individuals may spend their time getting the opinions of others or weighing their options. Because they spend their time engaged in these activities, they avoid making a decision.

Empathy: Empathy is an important trait in that it allows us to connect with others. However, it is important to control it sometimes during decision-making. We may believe that we know what others are feeling regarding the decisions that we are making. While it is important to consider how our decisions affect others, it is just as important to ask them how they feel about it rather than thinking that you know. Without verifying, our assumptions may make our decision-making harder than it has to be.

How to Beat Analysis Paralysis

Analysis paralysis, as with any thought or behavior pattern, can be changed if you know how to approach it. The following are suggestions for how you can do that:

Recognize Your Pattern: If you know what to look for, you can anticipate your analysis paralysis before it takes hold and make a shift to a more empowering way of thinking. Normally, when we need to make a decision, we use a short list of options we have available. What you want to avoid is going overboard on information gathering. Some examples of this are:

- When going online, you go beyond the first few tabs because you were not satisfied with the results on the tabs that preceded it
- You have a list of pros and cons that are more than 10 items long
- For making decisions with minor impact, you spend more than a day doing research
- You become obsessive in doing research, including during your free time

All of these are examples of ruminating over data. If you catch yourself doing this, put a stop to it. You will save yourself a lot of time and energy. Instead of doing additional research, figure out your next move.

Besides ruminating over data, also pay attention to what is happening with your body. Place your attention on your body, from head to toe. Do you detect any muscle tension? How is your breathing, shallow or deep? Are you experiencing nausea or any other signs of distress? Are you engaging in overthinking?

Set a Time Limit: Set a time limit for how much time you will spend doing research. Also, give yourself a deadline for when you will make your decision. There are a variety of ways to schedule your time:

- Block out time on your planner or calendar.

- Break down your research time into smaller installments that are of short intervals. Example: If you are going to schedule four hours of research, break down those four hours into 16 installments that last 15 minutes.

- Use a time-blocking app.

By limiting your research time, you will save time and energy as well as build self-discipline.

Remember the Purpose of Analysis: The purpose of data analysis is to gather information, to back up decision-making, or to support your concern for decisions made by others. However, problems occur when the analysis of data is influenced by feelings of fear, uncertainty, or indecisiveness. In an organization, you can add management discord as a negative influence. Data analysis can also be misused when the underlying reason for it is being used to create a hurdle, used as a crutch, or when it becomes politicized. These kinds of influences create analysis paralysis.

Stay True to Your Objective: Another way to be more effective in your decision-making is to know what your objective is and stay true to it. Staying true to your objective will help keep you from overthinking your decision-making process. Knowing your end objective will speed up your decision-making because you know what the goal is.

When making a decision, if the information is not relevant to achieving your objective, it should not enter your decision-making process. I recommend that you get clear on your objectives and continuously remind yourself of what they are.

Know What Your Priorities Are: The problem with overthinking the decision-making process is that it is taxing to the brain. Our brains become overwhelmed with information. When this happens, we lose our focus and get distracted by secondary or irrelevant information. The objective that we were trying to achieve is forgotten. For this reason, it is helpful to prioritize the decisions that you need to make.

Some decisions are difficult while others are easy. It makes sense that you want to save the most mental energy for you to make more difficult decisions. To do this, schedule your decisions so that you can balance them according to their level of difficulty. This can be done according to your behavior or work patterns.

If you are most alert in the morning, then handle your difficult decisions then and address the easier ones later in the day. You can also spread out your decision-making over your work week. Each workday, schedule one difficult decision and several easy ones to balance them out.

Practice Makes Perfect: You can improve your decision-making abilities by practicing making smaller decisions. As you practice making smaller decisions, you will gain insights into what your strengths are and where you can improve regarding decision-making. You can then apply it when making more difficult decisions.

The heart of overthinking is uncertainty; it is also the heart of us not being able to make a decision. It is the element of uncertainty that causes us to get stuck in the research process. Besides this, there is also the challenge which is that our decision-making is often based on our assumptions, which may not be true. In the long run, the only way to determine if our assumptions are accurate is to test them out by taking action.

The iterative approach is a method that you can use to test out your assumptions without committing yourself to going all the way with your decision. The iterative approach is a concept that was originally employed by emerging software development companies that had minimal resources. These companies performed extensive customer research to understand their customer. Despite this, the companies could not be sure how their customers would receive their products. They risked spending time and money perfecting a product only to find that the demand for their product was not there.

To resolve this dilemma, the companies focused their attention on creating a "minimum viable product." Releasing a "minimum viable product" allowed the companies to get feedback from their customers so that they could test the validity of their assumptions. They then could focus on making the needed adjustments on the next version of the product.

This same process can be used in your decision-making process. Instead of fearing that you will make the wrong decision, treat each step of your decision-making process as an experiment that you can test. If your decision does not work out as planned, you can make adjustments later.

Take Five: If you find yourself having difficulty making a decision, take a break. Temporarily remove yourself from the problem and let your mind clear. When you return to the situation, you may find it easier to decide on what you want to do.

Practice Deciding Quickly: If you are experiencing problems making decisions, practice making decisions more quickly. Start with small decisions that lack any significant consequences to you, such as what to wear in the morning.

Make your decisions quickly, without taking time to think about them. As you practice doing this, you will gain confidence in your ability to make decisions. You can then approach more impactful situations in the same way. Take a look at the facts and arguments for each option and then make a quick decision.

Get a Second Perspective: When we overanalyze a situation, we can lose all sense of objectivity. Try asking someone whom you trust what they think about your situation so that you can have a different perspective. If your situation is work-related, ask a coworker if they can briefly look into the situation and present them with a summary of your data. You can then ask them how they would approach the situation.

Remain Present and Limit Your Forecasting: One aspect of analysis paralysis is spending too much time thinking about how the outcome of our decisions will affect the future. While it is important to consider this, it is also important to realize that our ability to predict the future is iffy at best. Limit your projections of the future, focus more on the present moment, and move on to the next step. By making smaller and more intermediate steps, you can adjust as needed.

Become Friends With Uncertainty: Making big decisions can be difficult, especially when there are several favorable options. However, even when you have done all your research, sometimes you have to trust yourself and make a decision. No one can predict the future and all your efforts to gather information will not guarantee anything.

The element of uncertainty is a factor in most decision-making. Instead of contemplating your options until you feel a sense of certainty, befriend the feeling of uncertainty as a part of life. There comes a time when you have to trust your instincts after following legitimate decision-making strategies.

The Confidence Factor: Analysis paralysis may lead to developing low self-esteem, while low self-esteem can lead to analysis paralysis as we do not trust ourselves to make the right decision. Because we do not trust ourselves, we rely on gathering data. The way to break this vicious cycle is to build up your self-confidence.

One way of doing this is to work on overcoming procrastination. Analysis paralysis is a form of procrastination in that we are trying to avoid the perceived pain that we would experience if we made a wrong decision. Work on building trust in yourself. Believe that whatever the outcome of your decision is, you can deal with it.

Do Not Wait - Go for It: Those of us who experience analysis paralysis often believe that we do not have what it takes to make the right decision. We may tell ourselves that we have to feel ready before we can do so. The question is, how long will it take you to get ready? Also, how will you know when you are ready?

Sir Richard Branson is a business magnate who is worth $4.6 billion. He is the owner of Virgin Group, which oversees over 400 companies (Farkas, 2021). He started many of his ventures that involved fields he lacked expertise in, an example being space travel.

Branson did not feel prepared or qualified to handle many of his ventures. What he did believe in was himself. For many situations, who you are and what you know is enough to get started in what you need to do. This does not mean that you should foolishly rush into a situation thinking that you can handle it on your own.

I am an intelligent and well-educated person, but it would be a disaster if I decided that I could take the place of a surgeon or an airplane pilot. However, I do trust that I can learn what I need to know so that I can make an educated decision in an area that I am not an expert in.

Get the relevant information that you need and then trust yourself to make the decision that you need. You will always experience a certain amount of uncertainty when making a decision. Instead of dwelling in your uncertainty, dwell in the belief that you are good enough to make a decision. You will figure it out as you go.

Stop Searching for the Best Decision: Those of us who experience analysis paralysis often fall for the illusion that somewhere among our numerous web searches, there is the best decision for our situation. Just as we overthink the potential future outcomes of our decisions, we believe that there is the perfect solution. Such a solution is just a unicorn; it does not exist.

Each person brings unique variables into their situation. Our beliefs, our level of self-awareness, and our personal history are all variables that can influence the outcome. It is for this reason that there is no one-size-fits-all solution. The initial decisions that we make are less of an influence on the outcome. It is the days, weeks, months, and even years that follow that will provide us with the necessary feedback on where decisions are leading us to.

If we do not like what we see, we can always make changes in our decision-making. When confronted with a difficult decision, select the option that most motivates you as that is where you will apply your energy and time.

In the next chapter, you will learn about the different decision styles and tips for decision-making.

Chapter 6:
What Is Your Decision-Making Style?

"Truly successful decision-making relies on a balance between deliberate and instinctive thinking." ~ Malcolm Gladwell

We begin this chapter with two scenarios:

Scenario 1: You are sitting in a restaurant and are looking at the menu, trying to decide what to order. As you study the menu, you try to find the dish that comes closest to meeting all your criteria. Among the things you consider are:

- Price
- Calories
- Is it gluten-free?
- Do additional sides come with your order?

Scenario 2: You are sitting in a restaurant, and you take a brief look at the menu. You then look at the table next to you and are tempted by what they had ordered. You decide to order the same.

Which of these scenarios most accurately describes what you would do? When deciding upon your options, do you look for the best possible one, or do you go with the one that feels right to you?

Western society provides many of us with a seemingly endless number of options to choose from. Consider the choices that are available to you when you go to the grocery store, the car lot, or when shopping for fashion. You would think that having so many options would be a benefit. This assumption is reflected in the economic notion that as people, we approach our purchase decision in a rational and informed manner where we select the option that maximizes our needs.

This assumption became known as the "rational choice" theory. The rational choice theory states that we do not simply select products randomly. Rather, we use a logical decision-making process where we weigh the cost and benefits of our options.

Behavioral economists point to a problem with the rational choice theory. They argue that as our options increase, making a decision becomes more problematic. The first problem is that collecting the information to make a decision becomes more difficult. Second, as our options increase, so do our standards as to what is acceptable.

Lastly, we may start blaming ourselves if we are disappointed with our decision. We may tell ourselves that if we kept looking, we would have found the perfect option. However, not everyone finds themselves caught up in deciding amid the vastness of options. Why is that? Why do some individuals closely scrutinize the menu while others are fine just ordering what looks good to them? Also, which approach wins in terms of making the better decision? These questions were studied, with some surprising results.

Psychologists have identified two different styles of decision-making; maximizers, and satisficers (Psychologist World, 2023). When making a decision, maximizers strive to find the option that will maximize their benefits. Satisficers seek to find options that meet their needs. Let us take a deeper look at these two styles.

1. Maximizers

To begin with, both maximizers and satisficers will begin at the same point when it comes to decision-making. Both of these styles will search for the option that meets their basic needs. Where maximizers differ from satisficers is that once they find an option that meets their needs, they continue to look further for the option that provides the greatest benefits or utility. The following is an example: Let us say that Jim, the maximizer, is looking to buy a car. He is given three options:

- Vehicle 1 is a new car that is fully automated but is not fuel efficient.
- Vehicle 2 is a used car that is fully automated and fuel efficient.
- Vehicle 3 is a new car, slightly more expensive than vehicle 2. It is fully automated, fuel-efficient, and has tinted windows.

Most likely, Jim will choose vehicle 3. Though vehicle 3 is more expensive, Jim feels it would give him the maximum number of benefits.

2. Satisficers

While maximizers will prolong their decision-making process to find the "best" option, satisficers like to make their decisions as quickly as possible. They are looking for an option that is acceptable to them. Satisficers do not need to have a wide range of options or data.

While maximizers rely on amassed information and explore numerous options to make a decision, satisficers need fewer options, basic information, and their gut feeling. If such an individual was provided the same car options as Jim had, that individual would probably purchase vehicle 2.

It should be noted that individuals are rarely, if ever, all maximizers or all satisficers. Rather, think of these two decisions making styles as forming a continuum and most of us fall somewhere on that continuum.

More Is Not Always Better

Conventional thinking would suggest that the more you put into your decision-making, the better your outcome will be. For this reason, you may conclude maximizers enjoy a better outcome from their decision-making. Surprisingly, research demonstrates that it does not always work that way.

Research shows that maximizers often make less effective decisions than satisficers, and there are several reasons for this (Psychologist World, 2023). Maximizers create a lot of pressure on themselves because of the high expectations that they set for themselves. By setting such high expectations, maximizers prevent themselves from achieving their ultimate goal, to feel good about the decision that they made. They may feel that they failed by going for the option that they chose.

Rather than appreciating what they have, they may focus on what they missed out on. For this reason, maximizers are more likely to experience buyer's remorse. Satisficers, on the other hand, are more likely to be satisfied with the decisions that they made, even though they may not have been what they hoped for.

One study took a look at recent college graduates and the level of satisfaction with their decision-making as it relates to employment. Those graduates who scored high on maximizer tendencies found jobs with starting salaries that were 20% higher than those of satisficers. However, maximizers were less satisfied with their positions than satisficers (Psychologist World, 2023).

The researchers concluded that the reason for this discrepancy in job satisfaction was due to maximizers being more likely to second-guess their decision-making. They were more likely to think that they might have missed out on a better career choice (Psychologist World, 2023).

Maximizers are more heavily influenced by external factors. In their decision-making process, they rely more heavily on researching information about their options. They are also more likely to compare themselves to others, who they feel are more successful. Satisficers, on the other hand, rely less on informational research. They rely more heavily on what feels right to them.

Because of this, they are also less likely to compare themselves to others. In other words, both maximizers and satisficers are looking for the same thing when making a decision. They both want to feel satisfied. Maximizers invest a lot more time and energy in search for a satisfactory decision while satisficers simply go straight to it.

Which Is the Better Style?

So, which is the better decision-making style? There is no clear answer to that question. Rather than thinking one is better than the other, it is better to become aware of both of these tendencies within you and use the one that best fits the situation.

For most of your daily decision-making, using the satisficer style will allow you to make decisions that are satisfying and do not require you to invest a lot of time and energy. For high-stake decisions, you can use the maximizer approach by thoroughly researching the matter.

When you reach a decision, go back to the satisficer approach. Namely, be satisfied that you made the best decision given what you knew at the time.

Decision-Making 101

Life contains a feedback mechanism in the decisions we make. Our decisions lead to actions, and our actions lead to outcomes. The outcomes we experience are the feedback we are getting from life. If the outcomes we experience are positive, then we know that we made the right decision. However, if we experience an undesirable outcome, that does not mean we should judge or question ourselves. An undesirable outcome simply means that our actions did not align with the outcomes that we hoped for.

Your life is largely a product of the decisions that you made in the past. Much of what you experience today is the culmination of the decisions you made. In turn, the culmination of decisions that you make today will largely shape your future. At any time in your life, you can change how you make your decisions. Change how you make your decisions, and you will change your life.

The following are suggestions for making decisions more effectively:

As mentioned earlier, life is constantly providing us with feedback about the decisions that we make. Whether your decisions lead to success or failure, learn from the feedback that you receive as opposed to judging yourself. The more you pay attention to your feedback, the better the decisions that you will make in the future.

If your decisions did not turn out as you had hoped, reflect on what led up to your decision-making. Were your assumptions wrong? Did you get input from others? Did you react out of fear? What can you do differently in the future? By reflecting on what happened in the situation, you are utilizing the feedback you have been given.

The Importance of Self-Confidence: Self-confidence is a two-edged sword. It is important to have confidence in your ability to make good decisions. Without self-confidence, it is too easy to make decisions from a state of fear. You may have a history of making bad decisions, but you do have the capability to make good ones by learning from your mistakes.

On the other hand, there is a danger of being overconfident. By being overconfident, you run a risk of not questioning your assumptions. By not considering other perspectives, you may become blinded by your erroneous thinking.

Keep a Look Out for Your Heuristics: Heuristics is just a fancy word for mental shortcuts. Imagine that you are crossing a street when you see a car barreling down toward you. You could take a moment to try to analyze the situation to determine what you should do.

However, spending those few moments trying to make a decision could cost you your life. Fortunately, our brains are wired to provide mental shortcuts. Instead of trying to process the situation and figure out what is going on, these mental shortcuts allow us to reach a quick conclusion: Get out of the road!

Thanks to the brain's heuristics, we can come up with instant decisions for dealing with complex problems. By doing so, we avoid overloading our minds with information. When heuristics are used, the decisions we make may not be optimal, but they normally get us out of a situation when we have limited time to think the problem through.

Our minds do not resort to using heuristics only when we are faced with a threatening situation. They can be activated even when we are faced with mundane decisions. The role of heuristics is to save us time from having to think about something. Because of this, the use of heuristics can lead to distorted thinking, such as cognitive bias.

Heuristics causes us to respond to limited information. Going back to the scenario of you crossing the street, your brain is focused on the car heading toward you. It is not giving attention to any information other than that.

Under normal situations, that missing information prevents you from having any larger context for the situation that you are dealing with. If you read a psychology book on dysfunctional behavior, you will likely start seeing dysfunctional behavior in the people you know. Your mind took limited information (the book), and you assumed that is the reason why others behaved the way that they did.

Instead of rushing to judgment, try to identify what heuristics you use. Doing this will allow you to determine if you are allowing them to influence your decision-making. Identifying your heuristics takes time as they may feel natural to us. If you have trouble identifying your heuristics, pause before making a decision. Ask yourself, "Is there another explanation for what happened that I am not considering?"

Project Yourself Into the Future: When making an important decision, think long-term. Imagine what your life will be like 3 years from now, 10 years from now, 30 years from now, and so on. How may your decision today affect you then?

Step Outside the Box: More often than not, there are more alternative options than we may be aware of. Use your imagination and creativity to think about alternative options. For example, many young people who want to go to college are unable to afford it. They either decide to put off college or take out student loans. Instead of restricting oneself to these two options, one could find a job with an employer who will help pay for their tuition. Or one could go to a community college to take their prerequisites while working to save money so that they can attend their desired school later. Whenever you need to make a major decision, try to come up with alternative options.

Create Distance for a While: Sometimes we get so enmeshed in a situation that we can no longer see the situation clearly. Create some distance from the situation by taking a break from it. Do something different that will clear your mind. You can then return to the situation with greater clarity.

Treat Your Mistakes as Teachers: When making a decision, reflect on the mistakes that you made in the past when it came to decision-making. During those times, what did you do or not do that led to those mistakes? By learning from your mistakes, you can avoid repeating them.

Back It Up With Data: Learning to trust your gut instinct is a valuable tool in decision-making. However, your gut instinct should be part of your decision-making process. Whenever possible, look for data to support it.

Sometimes, our gut instinct is all that we have, and we have no choice but to rely upon it. However, your gut instinct may be faulty if it is based on psychological bias or other forms of distorted thinking. If your gut instincts tell you that you should quit your corporate job and become a photographer, find out what the demand is like in your area, what the average income is, and where the opportunities are. If the data supports your gut instinct, go for it!

Stay True to Your Values: What is the purpose of making a decision? The purpose is to choose the option that will give the best outcome. Why do you want the best outcome? You want the best outcome so you can be happy. Ultimately, all of our decisions are made to maximize our happiness. It is for this reason that you must make decisions that are based on your values.

As long as you make your decisions based on your values, you will have made the right decision. If you make a decision that goes against your values, you may receive many benefits, but none of those benefits will make up for your lack of happiness and sense of integrity.

If you value family, odds are that selecting a job that requires a lot of travel will not make you happy, regardless of how much you can earn. If you value excitement, you will not be satisfied if you enter a relationship with someone who values security. If you value certainty, you will not feel safe if you take a free vacation to a place you have never been before versus paying to go on a vacation to a place you are familiar with.

Before you can make your decisions based on your values, you first need to identify what your values are. On a piece of paper, write down the 10 things that are most important to you. Here is an example:

- Family
- Love
- Freedom
- Friendship
- Security
- Independence
- Money
- Adventure
- Play
- Connection

If the decision that you make is consistent with your values, you will have made the right decision. If your decision conflicts with your values, you will have made the wrong decision.

Recognize Your Biases: Our biases create distorted thinking, which leads to flawed decision-making. As with heuristics, biases are shortcuts that the brain uses to make quick decisions. We all have biases and understanding what your biases are will improve your decision-making. There are three kinds of biases; confirmation bias, sunk cost fallacy, and bias of overconfidence.

1. Confirmation Bias: Confirmation bias occurs when we focus on information that supports our current beliefs. Information that does not validate our beliefs will be discounted or questioned. For example, if you believe the government is corrupt, you will focus on media stories that support that narrative.

2. Sunk Cost Fallacy: This bias refers to when we continue to do something simply because we are heavily invested already. An example is someone who keeps investing money in a stock even though it has a poor return. Because they have invested so much money already, they keep hoping that the stock will go up.

   Another example is someone who stays in an unhealthy relationship. Even though they see no improvement in the relationship, they have already invested a lot of time and energy in it. They stay, hoping things will change.

   Stop making the same decisions for things that have a proven record of not working. Regardless of how much time and effort you have invested already, start making decisions that will result in actions that will improve the outcomes you are looking for.

3. Bias of Overconfidence: The bias of overconfidence simply means that we are so sure that we know what we are doing that we are not open to other viewpoints. Regardless of how much you think you know, it is advisable that you open yourself to the perspectives of others.

Emotions, Dogs, and Discipline: If you are knowledgeable about dogs, you know that dogs mirror their owner's level of awareness. Owners who do not provide discipline to their dogs will have undisciplined dogs. Such dogs will get anxious and fearful, leading to misbehavior. On the other hand, owners who provide their dogs with love and discipline have well-behaved dogs.

Our connection with dogs is based on emotions. When we are calm, our dogs will be calm. When we are emotionally reactive, our dogs will do the same. If you want to gain control of your dog, you first need to get in control of your emotions. Because of this, our dogs are a reflection of our relationships with our own emotions. Most of us are not masters of our minds. Rather, we allow our minds to master us. If we cannot take charge of our minds, how can we control our dogs?

We become better decision-makers when we learn to take charge of our emotions. To take charge of your emotions involves learning to not get caught up in them. You are not your emotions; you are the one who experiences emotions.

By creating distance between you and your emotions, you will realize that you can remain in charge regardless of what emotions arise within you. You can choose to not be reactive when they are experienced. When you take charge of your emotions, they will not get in your way when you are making decisions.

Get It Down on Paper: Writing down your thoughts is a powerful way to clarify your thinking, as we discussed earlier in this book. When you write down your thoughts, you are putting them on display, allowing you to make sense of them. Additionally, you bring relief to your mind because you are no longer engaged in rumination. Also, do not be surprised if you find that some of your thoughts do not make sense. Writing out your thoughts offers you a different perspective of your thinking.

Do a Cost and Benefit Analysis: While writing down your thoughts can be helpful in decision-making, there is also a more direct writing technique. You can do your own cost and benefit analysis. Get a piece of paper and create two columns. In the first column, write down all the benefits you expect that you will gain by making your decision. When doing this, include both short-term and long-term benefits.

In the second column, write down all the consequences you may experience from making your decision, again, including short-term and long-term. When you review what you wrote, determine which is greater, the costs or the benefits.

Once you have made a decision, take action. No decision is perfect. It is never too late to make changes if you see that your decision is not working out.

In the next chapter, you will learn about cognitive distortion. You will find out how our thoughts can sometimes distort reality.

Chapter 7:
Rethinking Your Thoughts

"Do not believe everything you think!" ~ Robert Fulghum

"Things never work out for me."

"What if I do not get the job? What if no one hires me? What if I become homeless?

"I cheated on my diet. That proves that I do not have what it takes to lose weight."

The above statements are a few examples of cognitive distortion. Cognitive distortions are patterns of thinking that are not fact-based. As a result, they can lead us to adopt a negative point of view of ourselves and others. In turn, this viewpoint leads to overthinking.

Your thoughts determine how you feel and what actions you will take. If you have a negative thought, it will show up in how you feel and what you do. The challenge is that your negative thoughts may not reflect the reality of the situation. Rather, your thoughts may be based on incorrect assumptions.

It is important to note that cognitive distortions are not a type of mental illness. Further, we all have them. When it comes to being an effective decision-maker, it is important to be aware of them so that they do not influence your decision-making. Chapter 1 covered a few examples of cognitive distortions. These included:

- All-Or-Nothing Thinking: Things are either right or wrong

- Catastrophizing: Thinking of the worse possibilities
- Overgeneralizing: Believing that because one situation is a certain way, all similar situations will be that way
- Jumping to Conclusions: Drawing conclusions about a situation without any supporting evidence
- Mind-Reading: Believing that you know what someone is thinking without any evidence

The following are other forms of cognitive distortion:

Personalization: This type of distorted thinking leads you to believe that you are responsible for events that are not your responsibility. As a reaction to feeling responsible, you may experience guilt or blame others. An example of this is a parent who allows their child to go on a camping trip. While on the camping trip, the child suffers a serious injury. The parent blames themselves for their child's injury because they allowed the child to go.

Another example of personalizing is when we believe others are responsible for what happens to us. Your partner asks you to do an errand for them. While running the errand for them, you get into a traffic accident. You blame your partner because if they did not ask you to do the errand, the accident would not have happened.

Control Fallacies: Control fallacies are cognitive distortions regarding our ability to control events. There are two kinds: Control fallacies and external control fallacies. A person may feel that they are somehow responsible for whatever happens to them or others. With external control fallacies, the person does not feel that they are responsible for anything that happens in their life.

An example of a control fallacy would be that you believe that you are responsible for how your partner feels. If they are upset, it is because of something that you did. An example of external control fallacies would be that you are running late for an important appointment, but you blame others for you being late. You blame your partner because they needed to talk to you, and you blame the person who called you at the last minute. Thus, your being late is due entirely to these happenings.

The Fallacy of Fairness: In this cognitive distortion, everything in life is judged by its level of fairness, according to your standards. If how you judge fairness differs from others, then you feel that they are wrong. The challenge with this is that things happen in life that have nothing to do with fairness; it is just the reality of the situation. The fact that COVID-19 turned our world upside down had nothing to do with fairness. It was simply a reality that we had to face.

Also, what determines fairness is not absolute as every person may have a different perspective on it. I may believe that it is unfair that the government spends my tax dollars on things that I strongly disagree with. Another person may feel it is unfair for them to have to pay any taxes.

Blaming: Blaming refers to when we hold others responsible for how we feel, which is a fallacy. While we cannot always control a situation, we always have control over how we respond to it. How we feel is something that we are in control of. When we blame others for how we feel, we are signifying that others have more control over our lives than we do. An example of blaming would be when I tell my partner that they made me upset because they did not do what they said they would do.

Shoulds: This cognitive distortion is very common in our society. The statements that we make about what other people "should do" or how things "should be" are the subjective rules that we impose on others and ourselves. Besides being subjective, our "should" statements often do not consider the specifics of the situation or the larger context.

An example of a "should" statement is: "People should always consider the feelings of others." While this is a reasonable expectation, it does not always work that way. Sometimes we may feel stressed and have a lot on our minds. During such times, we may be focused on our problems, making it more difficult to consider the feelings of others.

Emotional Reasoning: This kind of cognitive distortion results in us believing that how we feel about something reflects actual reality. An example of this is a person who feels inferior and does not believe that they have what it takes to be successful.

As long as this person believes this, they are likely to experience life this way. If they work to improve their self-esteem, they then will experience life differently. They will find reasons to be more hopeful. Reality did not change; what changed was how they felt about themselves. When that changed, their reality changed.

The Fallacy of Change: When we expect that others will meet our needs or wants, we are engaged in the cognitive distortion known as the fallacy of change. Even when we pressure others, they still may not do what we want them to do. A person may feel insecure and want their partner to spend time with only them.

However, their partner may have a sociable personality and enjoy spending time with others. They pressure their partner, telling them that they do not approve of their behavior. This person believes that by doing so, they can get their partner to stay with them. This kind of thinking is the fallacy of change.

Global Labeling: Global labeling refers to when we use an attribute to define the entirety. We can do this to ourselves and others by making sweeping judgments. For example, you may make a mistake or fail to attain a desired goal. Based on this single attribute, you tell yourself that you are a loser or that you will never be successful. Another example is that someone is late turning in a project, so you label them as being irresponsible. In both cases, a single attribute becomes a label for yourself or another person.

Needing to Be Right: When needing to be right becomes the most important thing to a person, they are likely to operate from this cognitive distortion. With this cognitive distortion, one's opinions are seen as facts. Such individuals will exert much energy to prove that they are right.

An example is in a relationship where one partner gets into an argument with the other over how they are irresponsible with their spending. The other partner believes that while they may have unnecessarily spent money at times, they are largely responsible. They also can point out times when their partner was irresponsible with money. Because their partner disagrees with them, the first partner becomes angry and continues to argue with them, even though it is making the situation worse.

Rethinking Your Self-Doubt: When cognitive distortions are not challenged, they can lead to self-doubt. Everyone experiences self-doubt at times; this is normal. In the right proportion, self-doubt can be beneficial as it can cause us to get motivated to work harder and improve ourselves. Years ago, I had self-doubt about my ability to be successful at work. Knowing that I could not afford to lose my job, I exerted myself to improve my job performance. Within a short time, I got up to speed with my abilities.

The problem occurs when our self-doubt prevents us from moving forward and demonstrating our greater potential. Common indicators of self-doubt include the following:

- You have difficulty accepting compliments from others, and you have difficulty giving yourself credit for the positive things that you do.
- You have a continuous need for reassurance.
- You experience low-self-esteem.
- You do not feel like you are good enough to achieve your desires.

Imposter syndrome is commonly associated with self-doubt. Imposter syndrome is a condition where a person feels like they are a fraud even though they may be successful. They have a problem acknowledging their achievements. This syndrome is commonly found in women and minorities (McFee).

Having imposter syndrome can prevent you from using your fullest potential and pursuing opportunities. Imposter syndrome commonly appears in the context of the workplace and relationships. The person will think they are not qualified enough or good enough for their job or in being a parent, partner, or other relationship role.

Ways to Overcome Self-Doubt

Self-doubt can be caused by numerous reasons. The important thing to realize is that the cause of self-doubt is less important than the ability to address it. The following are suggestions to help you overcome self-doubt.

Learn to Be Compassionate Toward Yourself: As the adage goes, to err is to be human. Being human means being imperfect; it means making mistakes. However, making mistakes is often viewed negatively. At a deeper level of understanding, one begins to understand that our mistakes are a gift, if we learn from them. Our mistakes provide feedback that our thoughts or actions were not aligned with our desired outcomes. By adjusting our thoughts and actions, we have a chance to hone them until they become aligned with what we desire. Demonstrate compassion to yourself by recognizing that you are going through a learning process, as we all are.

Remind Yourself of Your Past Success: There were times in the past when you doubted your ability to take on a certain challenge. Though you had doubts, you stuck it through and met that challenge. When you are doubting yourself, think back to those times when you overcame your fear and turned the situation into a positive. If you could do that then, you can do that now.

Stop Comparing Yourself to Others: The need to compare ourselves to others often comes from a sense of insecurity. More specifically, it comes from the ego, which is fear-based. The ego is on constant guard as it tries to protect the self-image that we have of ourselves.

By comparing ourselves to others, we make judgments of them. We are either better than them, or we are below them. Whenever you catch yourself comparing yourself to others, remind yourself that you are no better and no worse than anyone else. Each person is a unique individual who is equipped with their unique gifts and challenges.

Practice Mindfulness of Thought: Start paying attention to the thoughts that you are having. We have become so used to patterns of negative thinking that it may seem normal. Keep guard of your mind by checking in with yourself when you believe that you may be engaging in negative thinking. The more that you do this, the more aware you will become of your thoughts. You can then identify negative thinking when it occurs and replace it was more empowering ones.

Develop a Support System: Develop a support system of family members or friends who care about you and believe in you. Spend time with these individuals, especially when you are experiencing self-doubt. They can remind you of your strengths and offer encouragement.

Tame Your Harshest Critic: Who is your harshest critic? For most of us, it is ourselves. As mentioned earlier, it is important to make a shift from being your harshest critic to becoming more compassionate with yourself. Also, instead of comparing yourself to others, judge yourself by what improvements you have made and how you can continue to grow.

Keep a Journal: Keeping a journal is therapeutic as it allows you to write down your thoughts regarding self-doubt. By doing this, you will gain clarity and insights into thought processes, allowing you to address them in a way that supports you.

Talk to a Mental Health Professional: If you find that these techniques do not work for you, and your self-doubt is making it difficult to function in your life, consider seeing a therapist. They can provide you with tools to overcome your self-doubt. A popular treatment is cognitive behavioral therapy (CBT). By using CBT, you can learn how to effectively deal with problematic thoughts.

Limiting Beliefs: The Beliefs That Hold You Down

What we believe determines how we experience our world. You could say that beliefs are like tinted sunglasses. If you wear a pair of yellow-tinted sunglasses, everything that you see will look yellow. For this reason, it is not a reach to say that our beliefs create our experience of reality.

Since no two people share identical beliefs, it could be said that it is not possible to know the true reality. Each person creates their interpretation of what is true, based on their belief system.

For this reason, arguing whether a belief is true is less important than determining whether your beliefs support you or not in becoming happy. Our beliefs can empower us or limit us. In the following section, we will look at limiting beliefs.

What Is a Limiting Belief?

Throughout this book, the subject of focus has been mentioned. Our problem with overthinking has nothing to do with our thoughts. Our problem is that we are focusing on them. We are not only focusing on them, but we are also focusing largely on our negative thoughts. We overthink because we do not trust ourselves to make the right decision. We do not trust ourselves in making the right decision because of the negative thoughts that we have of ourselves.

When we have a sense of certainty that a thought is true, that thought becomes a belief. What you believe determines what you will focus on. Not only will it determine what you are focusing on, but it will also determine what information you will not pay attention to.

Self-doubt is created by the beliefs that we have which cause us to focus on our limitations while overlooking our successes. If you change your limiting beliefs, you will change your experience of yourself and your world. We can have limiting beliefs about anything in life. For convenience's sake, this chapter breaks down limiting beliefs into three categories, yourself, life, and our world.

1. Limiting Beliefs Regarding Yourself

This category includes any beliefs that you have about yourself that limit you in expressing your potential. The most common limiting beliefs for this category are the following:

- Age: This is the belief that you are too young or too old to pursue your desires.

- Personal Traits: These are the beliefs that because of certain personal traits, you cannot go for what you want for your life. Personal traits may include things like:
    - Your beliefs about your level of intelligence
    - Your beliefs about your physical appearance
    - Your beliefs about a physical handicap that you may have
- Emotions: Sometimes, we allow our emotions to form our limiting beliefs. The following are examples:
    - "I do not want to meet new people because I feel depressed. I will probably turn them off."
    - "I can never face them again because I feel so embarrassed by what happened."
    - "I am unable to have a healthy relationship because I am too nervous."

When our limiting beliefs are based on emotion, they can be particularly challenging to change. The reason for this is that the very thing that we need to do to change is the thing that we are resisting. The only way you can overcome your embarrassment is to face the situation and the people that are involved. If you are resistant to facing them then you will be fueling your embarrassment.

2. Limiting Beliefs Regarding the World

This category includes any limiting beliefs that you have about the world. An example of this would be the belief that you cannot trust others and that people will take advantage of you if given the opportunity. Common beliefs for this category include:

- Being Disapproved Of: We may limit ourselves in going for what we want if we fear meeting disapproval. Examples of such limiting beliefs include:
    - "I am afraid to meet people because they will think that I am a loser."
    - "I cannot pursue that field of work because of what my parents will think."
    - "I cannot leave my relationship because no one else will want me."
- Prejudice: Prejudice is an unfortunate reality of our world. Prejudice is created by the cognitive distortions that we have about races, genders, and other groups. While prejudice exists, you should not allow it to keep you from pursuing your best life.

    Prejudice thinking is often based on falsehoods. Even when the belief is true for a group, it does not mean that it will apply to every individual within that group.
- Being Full of Ourselves: While most limiting beliefs involve negatively seeing ourselves, some limit us because we think that we are special. Some of us think that we are too good for the rest of the world, so we hold back from pursuing our desires.

    An example of this would be someone who wants to become a musician but feels that their music would not be appreciated by the public because it is too sophisticated. Another example would be someone who has a vision for a business but believes that no one would understand their vision.

3. Limiting Beliefs About Life

This final category involves limiting beliefs that we have about our view of life. Some of the common beliefs for this category include the following:

- Missed Opportunity: This is the belief that you do not pursue your desires because you believe that you have missed your chance.

  An example is a middle-aged person who regrets that they did not go to college. In their mind, they feel it is too late to attend now. Another example is someone who has an idea for a product and decides not to pursue it as a business because someone else is doing it.

  The thing about missed opportunity is that it is usually illusionary. The middle-aged person may do better in an academic environment because of their maturity while the person with the idea for a product could find ways to improve it so that they have a competitive advantage.

- Time: Of all the kinds of limited thinking, the use of time to justify our limitations is probably the most common. This is not to say that time can be a real limitation for us; however, it is often overused. All too often, we hear people say that they want to improve their lives, such as exercising more or taking up an interest that they have, but they complain that they do not have the time to do so. If we want to do something, we usually can find the time! What we care about usually becomes the recipient of our time.

While we may be limited in our time, the time that we do have is often used ineffectively. Learn to prioritize your time. Those things that are most important to you should be scheduled. Get a planner and block out time for your high-priority items. If you have extra time, schedule the low-priority items.

Change Your Limiting Beliefs Into Empowering Ones

It was previously mentioned that we operate from a pain-pleasure dynamic. Everything that we do is to either avoid negative feelings or move toward positive ones. We adopt our limiting beliefs as a way to avoid pain.

If we do not think we can accomplish something, we avoid the risk of failure and being judged. Our limiting beliefs indeed cause us pain as they prevent us from growing as a person and trying new opportunities. However, the pain of risking failure is more real to our brains than is the abstract notion of achieving success in the future.

The good news is that we can use this pain-pleasure dynamic to our advantage by reversing the feelings that we associate with playing it safe. We can condition ourselves to associate pain with having our limited beliefs and pleasure in adopting empowering thoughts. The following are techniques for doing this:

What if Your Limiting Beliefs Are Wrong: Challenge your limiting beliefs by asking yourself, "What if I am wrong?" If your limiting belief is that you cannot afford to go to college, imagine in your mind that it is possible and think of ways that you could accomplish your goal. For example, could you apply for scholarships? Could you get a second job? Could you take one course at a time while you save money for a college fund?

Investigate How You Are Being Served: As previously noted, we do gain a benefit from holding on to our limited beliefs, such as avoiding the risk of failure. If we received no benefits from our limiting beliefs, we would not retain them. Ask yourself, "How am I being served by holding on to my belief?" When you identify what the benefit is, think about all the ways that holding your belief has cost you in the past. Then, think of all the benefits you would gain by replacing your limiting belief with a more empowering one.

Example:

Limiting Belief: "If I try to meet someone, I will be rejected."

Empowering Belief: "When I approach someone, it is a win-win situation. I will be accepted, or I will learn how to improve my approach."

By constantly reminding yourself of this, your brain will begin to associate pleasure with your new belief and pain with the old. When doing this exercise, it is important to focus on the feelings of pain and pleasure that come with having your beliefs. The final step is to start taking actions that are based on your new belief.

In the next chapter, you will learn about some of the common ways we fool ourselves through our thinking and what you can do about it.

How to Manage Your Cognitive Distortions

Overcoming your cognitive distortions is possible if you take the first big step, which is to become aware of them. Secondly, it is important to realize that, in most cases, it is not the situation that is bothering you but rather your thoughts about it. Overcoming cognitive distortions involves redirecting your attention from your distorted thoughts. The following are ways that you can take to deal with your cognitive distortions:

Check In With Yourself: Sometimes we experience anxiety or stress but are unable to figure out why. If this happens to you, it may be because you are experiencing a cognitive distortion. You may be able to alleviate the way that you feel by checking in with yourself and asking the following questions:

- Am I concentrating on the task that I am doing, or is my mind elsewhere?
- Do I feel tension in my body?
- Am I experiencing physical symptoms like a racing heartbeat, shallow breathing, or a stomachache?
- When did I first notice these signs?

Next, pay attention to the thoughts that you are having. Ask yourself if the way that you are thinking may be causing you to feel anxious. If you practice this technique, you will be able to identify the thoughts that causing you to feel stressed or anxious. The thoughts that you identify are the ones that you want to work on.

Identify the Biggest Troublemakers: This technique is similar to the previous one in that it will help you identify which negative thoughts you most often get caught up with. To do this exercise requires that you use metacognition, which is being aware of what you are thinking. To do this technique, you will need a journal where you can record your thoughts and moods. Do the following steps:

1. Each day, write down the thoughts that you experience most frequently. When recording your thoughts, be brief. Do not get into expanding upon them. Just write them down as they appeared to you.

2. Upon identifying a thought, try to connect the thought to a specific situation or place. Do this by asking yourself the following questions:

    - When did I first have this negative thought? Where was I when I had it?
    - How often do I think about it?
    - Do I have similar thoughts when I am in similar situations?

3. When you have made a connection between the thought and situation, identify the emotions that you associate with it.

4. At the end of each week, review what you wrote and see if you can find any patterns of thinking. For example: "When I am the focus of attention, I have the thought that I will blow it by making a mistake. That makes me feel like a failure."

Changing Roles: Without realizing it, I used this technique when I was younger. There were times when people said or did things to me, of which I was unclear as to whether they were acceptable or not. I did not have the highest self-esteem and sometimes tolerated behaviors, which I should not have.

One day, I had an insightful moment. Mentally, I replaced myself with my sister. I imagined that others were behaving toward my sister the way they behaved toward me. I then asked myself, how do I feel about the situation? Needless to say, I got upset. How dare they treat my sister that way! Because of this mind game that I played on myself, I quickly caught on to when I was being treated unfairly.

However, there is a twist to this technique. You can also use it to check on how you are treating yourself. I may have negative thoughts about myself, such as "You are not good enough." Because I am used to telling myself this, I may have lost touch with the kind of impact that this kind of thinking has on me. But what if I knew that someone whom I loved was having this kind of thinking about themselves? I would do my best to persuade them that those thoughts are nonsense and that I believe in them.

What I have just described is the technique of changing roles. Next time you experience negative thoughts about yourself, switch roles with someone you love.

Listen to What You Are Telling Yourself: Whenever you find yourself becoming upset about a situation, pay attention to what your internal dialogue is telling you. What are you telling yourself? I remember when I was driving when someone cut me off. I became angry at the other driver.

When I stopped to think about it, I realized that what bothered me was that I felt disrespected. I had taken the situation personally. As I thought about it, I realized that I did not know the driver, and the other driver did not know me. Further, he may have not been paying attention when he entered my lane.

Rid Your Thinking of Absolutes: Get over concepts such as "always" or "never" and replace them with words like "sometimes" or "maybe." Instead of thinking, "I always screw things up," tell yourself, "Sometimes I do not get things right." Instead of thinking, "He never listens to me," think, "Sometimes he does not appear to listen." Instead of thinking, "He is running late because he is irresponsible," think, "Maybe something came up that is causing him to be late."

Breaking the Cycle of Negative Emotions: Another way to deal with unpleasant emotions and repetitive thinking is to go step by step along the lines of your fears and take charge of them. You can do this by following this two-part process:

Part 1

1. Clarify what the situation is that is causing you to worry:

    - What is it that you are afraid of happening?
    - What may go wrong?
    - Who or what is causing you to have negative feelings?

2. Using your responses to these questions, imagine in your mind the situation happening to you. As you imagine this, really feel the emotions that you are experiencing. Think about the worst-case scenario. What is that? With this in mind, ask yourself the following questions:

- What is so bad about your worst-case scenario?
- What do you fear about your worst-case scenario?
- What are the outcomes of your worst-case scenario? How would they affect your life?

3. When you have found clear answers to the above questions, take a break for a few minutes. Do something to relax. When you are ready, ask yourself the above questions again. When answering your questions, use your original responses.

4. Repeat step 3, three or more times. Each time you repeat this step, try to go deeper into your answers.

Part 2

By continuing to repeat step 3 and getting deep into the emotion of experiencing your worst-case outcomes, you will have traveled from the beginning to the end of your fears. When this happens, you will come to realize two possible scenarios:

1. You come to realize that your fears were not as bad as you made them out to be. Your worst-case scenario was not as bad as you thought and you can survive it.

2. With clarity of what your worst-case scenario would be like, you can prepare for it instead of worrying about it. You will know what to look out for. Regarding this, ask yourself the following questions:

- What parts of my worst-case scenario can I control? Upon identifying these, determine what actions you could take to take control of your situation.

- What parts of my worst-case scenario are beyond my control? If you do not have control of a situation, there is no use worrying about it. Instead, learn to have complete acceptance of it.

Avoid Defining Yourself and Others: We are complex creatures, and we live in a complex world. Each one of us has a unique story, unique gifts, and unique challenges. With all this complexity, it's pure laziness to define ourselves and others by assigning a simple label. Who you are and those around you are more than a label. Instead of telling yourself that you are "not good enough," because you did not meet a project deadline, tell yourself, "I was not able to complete the project."

Look for What Is Positive: Whenever you experience a situation that you feel negative about, think about three things that are positive about it. When first doing this, it may seem unnatural but keep with it. At some point, it will seem natural. More importantly, it will keep you from becoming too negative, and it will give you a more balanced perspective.

Can You Prove It: Next time you experience negative or limited thinking, challenge its accuracy rather than blindly accepting it as being a reality. Question your thinking by looking for evidence to support it. Look for as much evidence that you can gather. Additionally, look for any evidence that goes against your thinking.

If you are having negative thoughts about a person that leads you to believe that they are selfish, look for as many examples as you can that support this belief. Then, do the opposite by looking for as many examples where this person did not act selfishly.

In the next chapter, we will explore how to create a lifestyle that will improve your decision-making abilities.

Chapter 8:
Developing a "Free Your Mind" Lifestyle

"Life is too short to spend at war with yourself. Practice acceptance and forgiveness. Letting go of yesterday's troubles is your first step toward happiness today."

This book has offered you a wide range of techniques to manage your overthinking. While techniques can be useful, sometimes creating the change that you are looking for is better served when you create a lifestyle change. Techniques are ways to do things differently; lifestyle changes are ways to live differently. The following lifestyle changes are effective for keeping a clear mind:

Develop an Empowering Morning Routine

What is your morning routine? Whether you realize it or not, we all have one. The question is, is it empowering? Before going any further with this topic, let us gain a better understanding of what a routine is.

Routines are a series of behaviors that we do to achieve a certain outcome. Your morning routine may consist of the following behaviors:

- Brush your teeth.
- Take a shower.
- Get dressed.

- Have a cup of coffee.

When you engage in these behaviors, you are being intentional in that you are telling yourself, "I need to do this to get ready." When we repeat a behavior enough times, it becomes a habit. Habits are behaviors that we do subconsciously, meaning that we do them without giving them much thought.

Any time we engage in new behavior, there is an altering of the neuropathways in our brains. You can think of this like the wiring in your home. You may have electrical cords running to different electric outlets so that you can provide power to your lamps, television, and stereo.

If you purchase a new exercise bike, you may have to rearrange the wiring to accommodate your new investment. The same thing happens when you engage in a new behavior. The wiring of your brain changes to accommodate the new behavior.

The more often that you repeat that behavior, the more effective the new wiring becomes in allowing that behavior to occur. There was a difference in what you experienced the first time that you rode a bicycle compared to what you experienced after repeated practice. The first time you rode, you were paying attention to every move you made as you tried to maintain control. After repeated practice, you just hopped on and rode away. You had to give little thought to what you were doing.

When we perform our routines enough times, our routines become habits. This is why after you perform your morning routine enough times, you no longer have to think about it. It is for this reason that changing our routines can be difficult. It takes repetition of the new routine before the new wiring in our brains takes hold.

If you change your morning routine to a more empowering one, and make it into a habit, you will change the way you feel about yourself and your life! The reason for this is that our morning routine prepares us for the rest of the day. If you have an empowering morning routine, that sense of empowerment will carry you through your day. Conversely, if your morning routine does not feel empowering, your sense of empowerment may be lacking.

The following are different suggestions for creating an empowering morning routine:

Being Organized: When creating your morning routine, it is important to get clear as to what you want. What would your morning routine need to look like for you to feel empowered? Let us say that typical mornings for you involve rushing to get ready and arrive at work on time. A more empowering morning routine may mean not having to rush and having some time to meditate, take a walk, or plan your day. Decide on the following:

- What do you want to gain from your morning routine?
- Develop a plan for how you are going to make it happen. For example, going to bed earlier and waking up earlier.
- Determine how you want to spend your extra time in the morning. For example, going for a jog or listening to music.

Commit to Your Plan: As mentioned earlier, it takes time before your morning routine will become a habit. In the meantime, you may find yourself struggling to make the needed changes. It can take up to three months for habits to form, so commit to following your plan. One way to stay committed is to remind yourself why you are trying to make changes to your morning. If you were successful in following your plan, what would you gain? How would it empower you?

Persistence: Persistence is needed to create change. Unfortunately, many people give up on making changes because they become impatient or become frustrated when they experience difficulty. One reason for this is that they take on more than they can handle. Instead, take small incremental steps by doing a little more each time you try to change your behavior. Be compassionate with yourself if you go off track. Stay persistent and let your brain do the rest of the work by rewiring your efforts into a new habit.

Develop an Empowering Evening Routine

We all have had nights where we cannot get our minds to become quiet and falling asleep seems impossible. You can develop an evening routine to help you decompress before going to bed.

A few hours before going to bed, do not use any electronic devices that emit blue light. What this means is that you should avoid watching television, or looking at your cellphone, or tablet.

Before going to bed, I recommend you do activities such as:

- Meditate.

- Perform deep breathing exercises.

- Write in your gratitude journal (which is discussed later in this chapter).

- Eat a low-carbohydrate snack, like popcorn, as such snacks will release serotonin, a hormone that relaxes the body.

If you still cannot fall asleep, try listening to audio tapes of white noise or get out of bed and engage in other activities such as writing or doing some light reading from a paper-paged book (remember these?)

Also, it is helpful to exercise during the day. You are more likely to fall asleep when your body has expended energy. Another thing that you can do during the day is to schedule worry time. Block out 15 minutes in your schedule where you permit yourself to worry. When your worry time is over, go on with your day. By scheduling worry time, you are less likely to hold on to them at bedtime.

Learning to Let Go

Ultimately, all of our problems, including overthinking, are the result of us not being able to let go. We hang on to the past, we hang on to our fears and pains, and hang on to our attachments. The point is that we hang on to our illusions. I say this because there is nothing in life that is permanent. Everything that we experience in life is transitory.

Our thoughts, emotions, and perceptions are constantly changing. Our bodies are constantly changing, and life is constantly changing. When we try to hang on to anything in life, we set ourselves up for frustration or disappointment. The following are suggestions for learning how to let go:

Create an Empowering Mantra: Create an empowering mantra that you can use to reframe a negative situation. Difficult times are bound to happen. Instead of giving in to negative emotions, develop a mantra that will remind you to let go. For example, "I feel blessed to be alive and that I can experience this moment," or "I am experiencing the cycle of life; better times are to follow."

Distance Yourself From Upset: Next time you experience a difficult situation, remove yourself from the situation. Instead of arguing with others, or resisting what is happening, distance yourself. Doing this will allow you to accept the reality of the situation. When you have gained acceptance of what is happening, you can think of ways to create value for yourself or others.

Take Care of Yourself: Any upset that you may experience was meant to be. We cannot control others; we can only control ourselves. Instead of resisting the experience, focus on caring for yourself by doing something that is nurturing.

Let Yourself Feel: Let go of the need to control how you are feeling. Whatever you are feeling as a result of a situation is what you are supposed to be feeling. Allowing yourself to feel what you feel is one thing. How you respond to your feelings is another. Allow yourself to feel what you are feeling but take responsibility for how you respond to them. It is okay to feel anger; it is another thing to do or say something that you will later regret.

Live With Acceptance: We are part of the universe, and the universe is part of us. At the deepest level, nothing in life is separate from anything else. The universe does not exist to meet our expectations. The universe operates based on what we consider to be fair or right. By learning to accept things as they are, you open yourself up to expanding your awareness, which is for your benefit.

As you gain awareness, you will develop the wisdom to respond to difficult situations that will benefit all stakeholders.

Cultivate an Attitude of Gratitude: Research has demonstrated that grateful people tend to be happier, healthier, and live longer (Harvard Health Publishing, 2021). The reason for this goes back to the power of focus. When we are grateful, we focus on what is going right in our lives rather than our wants or worries. Since there is a mind-body connection, the emotion of gratitude affects us physically as well. The following are suggestions for cultivating gratitude:

- Ask Yourself These Questions: Every morning and every evening, ask yourself, "What am I grateful for?" Follow this up by asking yourself, "Why am I grateful for it?" Lastly, ask yourself, "How does that make me feel?"

    When you ask those questions, focus on the feelings that you experience. If you have trouble coming up with a response to the first question, ask yourself, "What could I be grateful for?" and then ask the other two questions.

- Keep a Gratitude Journal: This is similar to the previous exercise, except it is done in written form. Each day, write down what you are grateful for. Additionally, indicate why it makes you feel grateful. The advantage of doing this is that you will be able to review what you have written in the past.

- Let Others Know: Each day, express your gratitude to someone you know. If you can, let them know in a card or letter.

- Prayer and Meditation: Each day, pray or meditate on gratitude. As you go within, think about what you are thankful for.

- Find Gratitude in Your Challenges: It is easy to be grateful when things are going well. We tend to forget about gratitude when faced with challenges. However, challenges can bring forth reasons for being grateful in ways that may not be evident to us, unless we look deeply into our lives. While challenges may create losses for us, they will create gains for us when we look at how our lives have changed.

I remember how I had relationship challenges, which led me to believe that I was not good enough for that person. Something happened in my way of thinking that caused me to stop trying to please them and focus on my needs instead.

Changes continued to occur within me, and I experienced a complete shift. I felt a strength within me that I never felt before. I also felt growing compassion for my partner. My initial challenge resulted in me feeling grateful for the growth that I attained.

Think back to the challenges that you faced. Can you find any benefits that you gained from them, that may not have occurred without those challenges?

By consistently doing the lifestyle changes mentioned in this chapter, you will develop routines that will become habits for you. These habits will help minimize overthinking as you will be providing your mind with a structure that is predictable to it.

The Journey Beyond the Last Page

Dear reader,

Thank you for embarking on this journey with me, exploring the corridors of the mind, and finding ways to navigate the maze of overthinking. As you close this book, the journey is not truly over; it is only just beginning for many others, seeking the tools and solace you have discovered.

Your personal insights can be the lighthouse for someone else drowning in a sea of relentless thoughts. By sharing your genuine and honest perspective of this book on Amazon, you guide countless others to the shores of understanding and peace they have been yearning for.

Scan to leave a review

Being an independent author, every piece of feedback is pivotal. It shapes the discourse, illuminates the narrative, and aids the success of the message I am hoping to convey. If you find a moment, I would be immensely grateful for your review on Amazon. I promise each word will be read, valued, and cherished by me.

Every sentiment, be it words of encouragement or constructive insights, are treasures in this shared odyssey.

With gratitude and anticipation,

Dean Bishop

Conclusion

The purpose of this book was all about providing techniques to manage overthinking. While these techniques work, it is important to view them as tools, not solutions. As with any challenge that you may face in life, the ultimate answer is you, more specifically, how you use your mind.

When a musician and record producer come together, there are two approaches that they can take. The first approach is to let the marketplace and the music charts shape the direction that the record takes. The second approach is not to give any attention to what is happening outside the studio. Instead, a complete focus is placed on what feels right to the musician. It is the job of the musician to present music that feels real to them while the producer helps shape that vision.

The same is true with overthinking or any other challenge that we may face. What is important is that you place your focus on what feels true to you, not what others may think. This does not mean that we disregard what others may say. We learn by listening to others. However, there comes a point when you have to do what feels right to you.

Overthinking is caused by overly focusing on what others may be thinking or fears of what may happen if things go wrong. This is not the kind of focus that leads to success. If success is a calm mind and a feeling of well-being, then your focus needs to be what feels right to you.

When you do this, you are being true to yourself. Since everyone has a different perspective, each person will have their own truth. Because of this, do not look outside yourself for your truth, look within instead.

About the Author

Dean Bishop, a prolific writer with a knack for delving deep into the human psyche, seamlessly weaves his own experiences with the struggles of everyday life to guide readers toward emotional freedom. For Dean, life has been a series of lessons learned through introspection and genuine self-awareness.

Growing up in a bustling city, Dean often found himself lost in a whirlwind of thoughts, seeking solace in the written word. His early fascination with literature and the intricacies of the human mind laid the foundation for his future writings. Dean's profound exploration of life's complexities led him on a transformative journey. It was during these moments of intense self-reflection that he honed his ability to translate these experiences into impactful narratives that resonated with many.

Throughout the years, Dean traveled extensively, absorbing the diverse cultures and philosophies from around the world. These travels enriched his understanding of human behavior and the universal threads that connect us all. Drawing inspiration from the myriad of people he met and the stories they shared, Dean became a beacon of hope for those wrestling with their inner demons.

With a sincere desire to inspire and uplift, Dean Bishop has dedicated his life to assisting others on their quest for clarity and inner calm. Apart from his written contributions, Dean is an avid photographer, capturing the fleeting moments of life that often go unnoticed. In his leisure, you can find him hiking scenic trails or engrossed in a riveting novel, constantly seeking knowledge and inspiration. Always a seeker of tranquility, Dean's writings reflect his own journey and are a testament to the power of perseverance, self-awareness, and genuine connection.

References

American Psychiatric Association. (2020). "Rumination: A Cycle of Negative Thinking."

Eng, C. P. (2020). "Think + Think + … Think = Overthinking." Articles of Teaching and Learning in Higher Education Vol. 1

Farkas, J. (2021). "Richard Branson Net Worth 2021: How Did He Make His Money?"
Go.Banking Rates

Glen, D. (2014). "Who Gets the Most Out of Cognitive-Behavioral Therapy for Anxiety Disorders?" PubMed.

Harvard Health Publishing. (2021). "Giving Thanks Can Make You Happier."

McFee, A. (n.d.). "Letting Go of Imposter Syndrome's Grip on Women & Minorities." EHL Insights.

Psychologist World (2023). "Maximizers vs Satisficers: Who Makes Better Decisions?"

Witmer, S.A. (2023). "What Is Overthinking, and How Do I Stop Overthinking Everything?"

Printed in Great Britain
by Amazon